sublingual
bill bissett

talonbooks

Talonbooks
P.O. Box 2076, Vancouver, British Columbia, Canada V6B 3S3
www.talonbooks.com

Typeset in Helvetica and printed and bound in Canada.

First Printing: 2008

The publisher gratefully acknowledges the financial support of the Canada
Council for the Arts; the Government of Canada through the Book Pub-
lishing Industry Development Program; and the Province of British Colum-
bia through the British Columbia Arts Council and the Book Publishing Tax
Credit for our publishing activities.

Library and Archives Canada Cataloguing in Publication

Bissett, Bill, 1939-
     Sublingual / Bill Bissett.

Poems.
ISBN 978-0-88922-589-3

     I. Title.

PS8503.I78S89 2008   C811'.54   C2008-903033-8

sum uv thees pomes apeerd previouslee in capilano review
precipice todd swift msundrstandings
sublingual th pome   wch was writtn 4   eVOCativ festival
universitee uv saskatchewan   saskatoon   june 08   was performd
ther with adeena karasicks econohomonymy: a poetiks of ethos,
eros and erasure simultaneouslee as th combind work sublingual
bouche   editing by adeena karasick

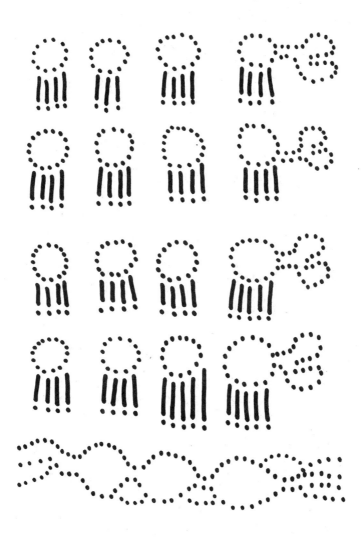

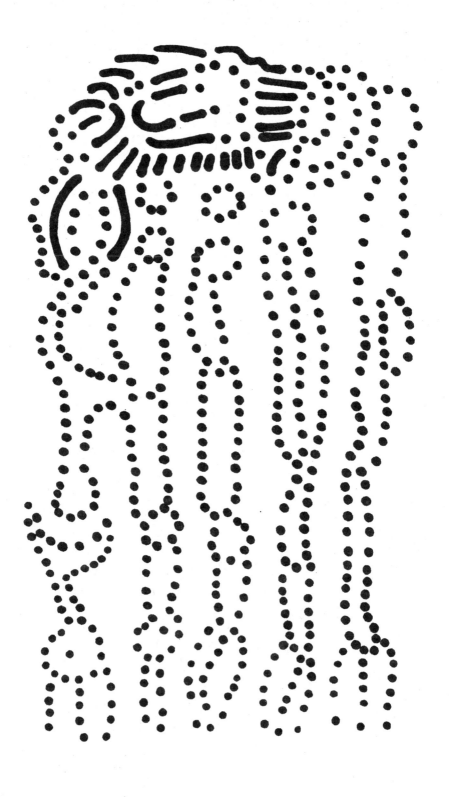

thers sumthing sew familyar abt life

mor thn i evr realizd at first breth had i
bin heer b4 that was my qwestyuning
                              feeling

as i made my way tord my
destinee i was alredee in
th pickshurs   was that it

looking 4 a love 2 hold on 2 2 b with
was it onlee inside me th pay off n sew
 veree familyar it all was   as

if i alredee belongd

what wud reelee help

is if president bush n his entire

kabinet wer arrestid
4 war crimes konviktid n all

givn life sentences

without chance uv parole

thats what wud reelee help

love

is gingr
is data base
is trembling
cellulose
is th big
bang bang
yr alive

mark i came upon thees lines
ystrday n i thot yu mite like
them n i definitlee thot uv yu
yu know iul b home monday

cant wait 2 grab yu my independent
spirit n 2 sleep with yu spend th nite
with yu all th brite darkness roll

ovr us dew yu want 2

sumtimes yu can wundr what i wundr th
north

sew brite 2nite th milkee way tall grass breething
sumtime yu sumtimes kreetshurs uv habit undee
velopd prototypes wer not reelee filld in yet   ants
2 gods eye still in th xperimental stages have we
bin kreeatid as a way on 2 sumthing bettr a diagram
thats stuk with life as th goal what if we wer 2 live
it all uv th time sted uv thinking abt it meeting in
kommiittee 4 th ovrview

dreem possibiliteez spontaneitee n knowledg not
evr reelee joining veree well robots n souls likewise
an intrlewd til th reel thing happns what is th reel
produktivitee ths is th reel thing ths moment yes ownd
n kontrolld by elites using poor workrs in developing
countreez if not now i wanna b frends not we build
our tomb 2gethr sumtimes imprisond in yr sound
sumtimes yu ar in mine whos is whos is it bcums lust
onlee wher yu turn away from a life anothr baloon
bust eye need mor patiens

spirit walk up north yu nevr know yr hung til yr
hanging in th fir treez seeing th animals eyez piers
th darkness in th clouds nowun can find us xsept
th great blu sky

evree brain is diffrent   if life is a cawsyunaree tail
what is it preparing us 4   duz aneewun know uv
kours not dew yu heer that sound in th bush th

sound uv bells in th wind

emerald elmerad meradel led rema

mald erla dalmelra merel erlam ald
era ermeld daire deira ad a ada mald erla

emerald   eme rid emerald emer ald
ermreld relda da ad da ma am ada mera mera

eldar elda ree aled led dale eer delda melda

emald alda aaaaaaaaaaaaaaaaaaaaaaaaaaaaaa

IIIIIIIIIIIIIIIIIIIIIIIIIIIIIIIIIIIIIIIIIIIIIIIIIIIIIIIIIIIIIIIIIIIIIIIIIIIIIIIIIIII

dddddddddddddddddddddddddddddddddddddddd

eeeeeeeeeeeeeeeeeeeeeeeeeeeeeeeeeeeeeeeeeeeeee

rrrrrrrrrrraaaaaaarrrrrrrrreeeeerrrimmmreemmeee
darma rama rame ddd dere   dare dareeeeeee
merl merld merlda e merla erlm me em eral

ma am da mmmmmmmmmmmmmmmm el al

mal lam ml dl el delm a rale ree elda relda a

melda delda eldam elmad lemda   leraldama mer

meer leer amer lader reem leem dera erad era

era d d ared dera mera lera eral dame am

de d d del ared dera meer lera eral dame am

era d mald maed meda mel el mead adme
dreem lemda denad damel eramdel d d   d

life is sew strange isint it sumtimes it is sew
compelling oddlee fascinating sew much uv
it is in retrospekt is it escapism what dew yu
think n from what n sumtimes it reelee hurts
dusint it   n sumtimes heels

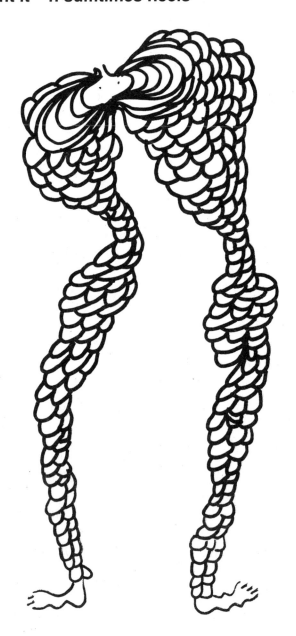

ystrday in th craydul uv th nite my lungs wer
having th deth rattul i woke up told my lungs
2 stop that cut that out it was way 2 skaree i
told them   n they stoppd

th emerald ponee

dew yu see it running
across th soggee medow
just b4 sun up skarlet n
gold th silvr dew still on

th aspen buds unfurling
in2 leevs its going 2 b
day soon n th emerald
ponee will make it deep
inside th bush 2 camoflage

with th inkreesing green
in time until nite fall whn
he can roam agen n run with
th foxes swallows th nite
birds

in wintr th emerald ponee
is white n is hard 2 see in
th snow standing foraging
4 straw undr th ice

i love getting up erlee n
seeing th emerald ponee
getting home soon b4
discovree it nevr looks

worreed tho its always
in synch in tune with th
harmoneez uv th magik uv
erth place th awesum tempo

uv th changing lite n dark

we humans peer thru

n see shining jumping n shy
th emerald ponee what
was that word th lettrs
falling like peesus uv shinee
gold out uv our hands
                        ands
                    n lands

th emerald ponee lies down
in it needs 2 dreem as well
as us dreeming uv th emerald
ponee n its suddn love n care
4 us n th mysteree uv being

knok knok whos ther th
white ponee genius uv
destinee n change running
thru th white orange field
stops n stares at us

n th erth shivrs b4 ice forms
n we run out 2 embrace th
white ponee b4 it races off
2 rock in2 th nu day evn th
suddn transe uv being n th

low lite hovrs n nobodee knows
nowun has seen th emerald
ponee 4 a few yeers now   oftn
devoteez stand hiddn in th
freezing snow 4 hours or in th

fiers spring winds waiting

as now it is known ther ar 2
poneez wun in wintr th othr
in spring sew ther ar 2 poneez
as well as th changing wun sew
ther ar three

poneez n th 3 cudint get 2
gethr at th same time n th
first emerald ponee was b
cumming sorrowful 4 th

behaviour uv human beings
its heart was breking 4 all
uv us nevr lerning us always
fiteing n nevr reelee changing
from that n th natural world

uv th emerald ponee was
starting 2 stink   it felt sew
horribul it impaled itself on
a sidewayze icikul thrust
out uv th frozn lake

n th othr 2 emerald poneez
cud nevr find each othr each
sew seesun dependent n
theyr hearts bcame brokn n

they drownd in th blood uv
theyr artereez bursting

ths is a part uv what peopul
have dun 2 th beautiful
natural world on bhalf uv

theyr divisiv delusyuns n
destruktiv thinking

writtn with jordan stone

he phond in n sd

he had had a prostrate
operaysyun n th doktor
sd take three months
b4 trying 2 get hard

sew he sd it was three
months now n cud i
have phone sex with
him

uv kours i sd in th
interests uv science
almost aneething

sew dot dot dot
dot   dot dot dot

my gowd he sd it
all workd   thats
great i sd   yes

great

yu feel love 4 a whil

thn insecuriteez thn th
angr 4 that n on 2 th
loving agen skratch yr hed
why duz it go th loving

n thn yu lick wounds rekluse
hide out catch up within
build around yr heart thro yr
self in2 yr work

each time th love goez
yu cry out cry in reelee thn
xperiment with holding yr hed
up carreeing on dewing tasks
work is reelee sew important

wun morning yu wake up n
realize yu ar in love agen

n evn tho yr skard a littul bit
sumtimes yr just sew happee

yu shud moov heer yu sd 2 me
i sd i will

i hope n its starting agen
all th unravelling love all th
tuffness is dissolving rivrs uv
trust humming in my heart

evreething

that goez in my
hed i put ther

what abt fakts
i sd 2 stuffus

him having xplaind
2 me that ther

was no reel word

world whirling

was it all sew
relativ words arint things

i sirtinlee have
relativs in nova

scotia n bc
n boston n
alberta n things ar things

wisconsin n
inverness how far
back dew yu want

is that subjektiv
life is strange eye

agreed that was

th thot th day b4
ystrday it is strange
n passing n what is
lasting iul miss
life words change

it wud b chagrining
if it werent mor thn
circutree n digestiv
systems things change

yu can feel yrself
letting yrself b happee
n whethr its domestik
or serching fluid

yu cum out uv th shadow

thers 2 much in my hed
agen i bcum closr 2 th
well th lake watr my
hed empteez feels each
rivulet currents still
ness loons swim in

thru my reseptors
closr 2 my eyez
look out change
changes n th

treez ar on fire
reflekting th sun
setting th deer
n me watching

th origins uv life love us

thers 2 much in my hed agen inklewding th rocks

th lyrikul line mooving thru fields uv chattr

halifax boy

in th moovee theatr
watching doris day
singing ten cents a
danse in sumbodee
loves me with james
cagney

i was flashing whn
i grow up i want 2
b a hookr

n i did n got mor thn
10 cents a danse it
didint work 4 me
4 long tho i was
alwayze wanting
trew love

n how much hardr that
was 2 find evn 2 touch
n hold 4 a whil

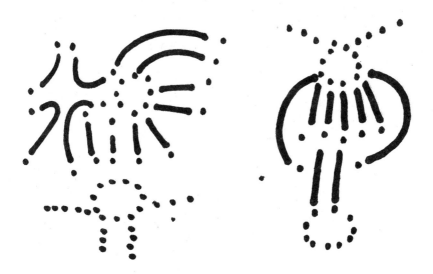

langwage n desire

thers mor 2 life thn being

thers also bcumming n

all th time yu have ar being
n bcumming

all th time ther is sperm
egg n sparrow

bone air
breeth th
pine n

erth loamee
desire names
4 evreething

cum with me sail ovr th horn
n th melting arktik names 4
places n feelings emerg n

erode change with th speekr
n th times   alphabets uv

being bcumming n not with th
partikuls uv touch meeting lick
turn sew tord n away from th
fire in th bellee change ash n
 goldn lite

n no names 4

polar bears on yonge street

sew ms lise n me wer going up
yonge 2 see how far it goez its sd
2 b th longest street in th world
on ths day aneeway we went north

on yonge street past th 7,ooo blok
past th turnoff 2 barrie wch was
still calld yonge street sew long
n we saw manee polar bears swetting
n hedding south as theyr arktik home
was melting we witnessd th polar

bears discussing among themselvs
what 2 buskr first look i sd 2 lise
its th polar bears on yonge street
soon theyul b down town in all th

terribul traffik yes she sd its cum
ming soon what will it feel like i
askd

itul feel like dying she sd or th
last circus

mark was writing 2 jim abt

les anges perdu nous sommes sa   vraiment jim
   sighd anothr stage in th development goin fastr
   n slowr all th time walk around th lake go thru
   th feer let it go whn th lovr bcums th othr its sew
painful sew manee peopul want 2 b king n qween
   n ther arint enuff thrones or chairs 4 them trubul is
can b whn men get 2 gethr aftr a whil ther needs 2
b a duel veree oftn tho thers sum women i know
th same way   powr is powr maybe   stiks swords
making bettr marks in th endless disapeering sand

ths is th realizasyun yes yu ar tuff enuff 2 not have it
mattr wun moment mor cut at a time n th goddess
is caring 4 yu me 2 b a hermit without physikul love
past ths next finish linr may not b possibul 2 go on
   yuve out manoeuverd yrself yu ar sumwher it is
   kool sew uv kours fine 2 b n thn wun nite in a
luvlee hotel room th pain on th rite side mattrs
th brain spreds   ice

brokn glass speeks brokn heart lost in that drifting
   brain cells reasembul with mor interesting qwest
yuns   is ths what happns 2 lost angels needing
warmth   sew much n sumwun touching yu how long
can th othr go on missing what yu cud give n take
hold n carree on with 2gethr if th pain goez it dusint
   mattr but b4 th pain came i felt it was long enuff or
   not 2 long what els cud happn why cud i not
physikalee endure   th powr sessyun well 4 startrs its
   not reelee interesting i need

a round carvd woodn box 4 my travls a south
western moon 2 guide me take me 2 th love
i dreem uv at nite b4 going 2 sleep sew hi on th
mountin angel time angel being climb in2 th stars
n grab th laddr spred yr doubts n feers sew far
out uv yu diamond droplets in th umbrella bowl
sky th stars ar it may b time 2 xploor th othr
world th each painful breth a littul easier heer
tho i lernd sumthing jim yu may b still hurting
from not finding a partnr yu may with a lovlee
strangr no longr strange at all n th realizasyun

it cant go furthr well 4get abt it it can go furthr
n may b with me if yu can trust enuff in yu yrself
yes how happee yu can b thn running 2gethr across
      th citee its a long n beautiful dreem keeps yu
          heer in th reel time world each heet each beet
each beet is free n melanges with our realizing
signal tunnels n limitid 2 th time its built 4 huh n n
n   needs not as much as prhaps yu thot th ancien
accident uv going on n on byond change evr
      byond dangr dangr yet still heer a stopling cums
n anee way yu me dont kontrol it yu can love it yr
    self massage it breeth it n dew with pleysyur uv
th pain getting less th longr yu can stay heer n fulfill
yr starree moonby see a mountin grass love n

finding th safetee n health uv being singul is sew
   fine nobul adventurous fun n loving a is just as
   gud as aneething els th teems uv arrows n wethr
vanes n walking thru a barrage uv barking dogs
      drool dropping off theyr bleeding teeth n gums
   theyr knarling if not wake th ded sure disturbs
   them a lot   yes n th vestibule sailing ovr th bougan
villea o my she sd i herd her reelee th barn hasint

bin th same sins th murdr n now its 4 sale end
uv an era reelee sumwher yu cud go dansing anee
  nite no dress code whatevr iuv seen th tunnul 2
4evr twice i sd can i finish my current program uv
work can i find love agen love is in th mediteranean
see uv yr mind yes turning warmlee 2 th parade
uv see horses

                        trampling ovr th bord walk n th
  nite hevnlee salt air what els cud it b paying atten
syun prhaps th time agen defeerd th bruis going 2
anothr place aftr it warms me dont live without
. love jim if yu cant find it with me pleez make th
attempt dont live without love howevr yu find it els

  yu wunt see th tigrs danse n th moon spin dont let
yr heart b brokn spin thru th april sky n th time uv
th erthee changing each orange n lunarian soup
  with th lentils n th lavendr scents enklosing yu
letting yu as yu leep from projekt 2 projekt loving yu
  fullee loving yrself

                        evn if its mor thn an intrim th
pirouetting oystrs n what am i missing n blankits
  warming n letting go uv th   sorrows hold yu neer
th fire n th   moonlee grace

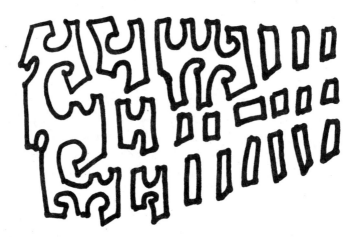

28

ium not a raptor a terradaktyl a tree

cant yu see ium a mammal   ium a mammal
with a heart beeting stuk in sircumstances

looking 2 finish th laundree whil waiting 4 a
guest 2 apeer th guest n th laundree ar on   far
diffrent floors whil ium puttin in th laundree is th
alredee veree late guest arriving at th front door oh
th angst uv it
                              ium th ghost on th third floor iuv
had sew much life my eyez staring out ovr th
balkonee in2 th fervid n obscure dark nite

yet i can long 4 mor   n ium happee
                                         n ium happee

ium th ghost on th third floor
each day is a mirakul   howd it get heer
ium kompleetlee surprizd   each morning i
get up n sit   meditate n let go   uv
evreething i can 2 prepare 4 th nu day   n ium
                                                     happee n
                                                     ium happee
heers anothr murmur from th paintrs
                                             tent   hey did
yu eet that sound did yu heer that kolour did
yu feel th angel breth

i did diffrent doors diffrent   floors diffrent timez a wind
blows thru i have my own resources   dont need 2
wait on th mystree guest yes th guest nevr arrivs n
i caut a chill airing out th room   4 th guest
who nevr   came

29

a hous in a landfill is a landfill

a troubuld time with th stars
mercuree in retrograde

a hous is a handfill

i thot uv thees lines whn nite
b4 last i xperiensd such a zanee
nite uv xtreem doubt th stars
wer unkonvinsing 2 me

can yu handul that in me its sew
cornball yu know i havint felt
ths way b4

i know i may not b what yu need

ar we still on 4 wednesday yes

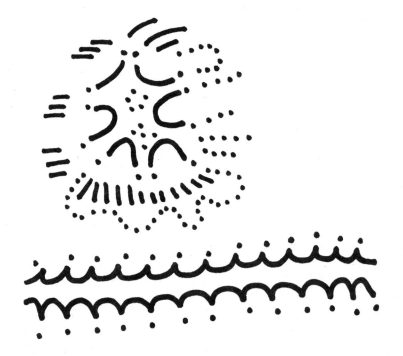

claire sd 2 me whn

things ar 2 gud 2 b
trew they usualee ar

its romantik
2 b doomd

opn th windo
n thers anothr
closd window
until until
until until

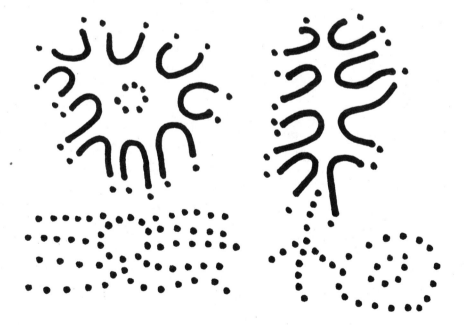

in jims lettr 2 mark he askd whn

they wud see each othr agen   how he thot uv
him sew much whethr he was working on th
konstruksyun uv th hous down th street wher th
blu spruce n th britest green pine treez wer
wrapping themselvs around th homes ther or
workin on his post graduate thesis on th brain
how infinitlee self heeling it reelee is how opn
th brain is 2 wider wiring we all cud enjoy wer
we 2 beleev mor in its mirakulous enerjeez
jim wud think uv mark almost all th time   as

his brain his hed was with him a kontrast 2 th
multitudinous multiplisitous being uv th brain sen
trs all ovr th brain such as th sentrs we bring 2 th
organizaysyun uv beleefs wer thot 2 komplement
now undr standing th selebrating th infinit reech
n dynamiks uv th brain lettrs all ovr n thru it yes
as th rivrs uv being run thru evree wher our
bodeez karree our brains or heds ther is no sentr

yet he onlee mostlee thot uv mark a strange n
wundrful n pulling uv th elastisiteez sew ther as
place he was writing 2 him wher he felt fullee alive
in being all ther n th watchrs who had oftn alwayze
bin with him 4 yeers n he was onlee grateful 4
that wer with drawing 2 look upon n help sum othrs
 n jim was sew realizing n saying 2 mark his place
among all th fluiditee n change was with him

th wun n th manee th wun in2 th manee th manee
in2 th infinit th thredding th mewsik uv th tapestree
we ar all inside evn with th vast n intrikate diffrenses
n similariteez n enhansing n shredding n change n

embraysing uv all th narrativs cud that b
r yu thinking uv me or if i can say us or me
in anee uv thees wayze

th gift uv time

evreewun wants sum kind uv trubul in theyr lives
he sd n ths is th kind uv trubul i want

eye went down 2 th beech

last nite lookin n an invisibul

vois sd its not xcellent
4 me 2 b ther

ium no fool

i walkd back home
immediatlee

mirakuls n our sumtimez goldn lassitude

th tenor uv tendrills waivd th purpul
wrinkuls n labyrinthean envelopes uv
bordr town wher he hoped wuns agen 2
fall in love n find sum time within sum

qualitee projekts n as th half moon seemd
2 turn ovr th scotia bldg in toronto his
frend was working on th 3rd draft uv a
lettr 2 him wher he told him agen uv his
love 4 him if he cud onlee possiblee have

th time 2 rekonsidr his plight emosyunalee
n his veree redusd sircumstances his hands
n fingrs found his own nippuls th xakt way
his frend had dun n he went out looking
reelee 4 his frend n in th morning whn th

replacement prson left he saw his frend
in his minds eye onlee mor kleerlee n
how he lovd him n his lonleeness in his
present situaysyun onlee inkreesd

dont look 2 hard

        sew ths psychik who came 2 t th othr day
she sd its time 4 yu 2 live with sumwun i sd what
makes yu say that

        n she sd i can reed it in yr aura i can reed
it in th stars i can feel it in th full moon passing ovr
our heds ovr mars n i know just th guy 4 yu

    i sd reelee dew yu how tall is he n she sd hes quite
tall n hes in yr area uv chronos hes veree brillyant
hes looking 4 sumwun 2 what makes yu think that

    n she sd i can reed it in yr aura i see it in th stars n
th full moon passing ovr us ovr mars sew ystrday she
phond n sd by th way th misyun i was telling yu abt
next week ium bringing him 2 see yu tuesday is gud

sew its like i cant stop it let happn whats gonna happn
i secretlee feel weul not get along its not like weul not get
along yu kno what ium saying tho i dont know that as
sew whatevr th psychik sd as long as ium up 4 it iul dew
it i dont think thats going with authoritee thats goin with
an insite isint it but dew i reelee want 2 live with sumwun

    duz aneewun kno but th psychik sd i red it in yr aura
i saw it in th stars i felt it in th full moon passing ovr us
ovr mars

        tuesday is gud veree gud

dew yu evr think uv how

varied n changing evreething reelee is
ths streem had me writing n painting 4
mor thn a few dayze n nites reelee almost
along sum sure or sirtin lines or currents
yes i was sew in2 it like being in a 4ward
rivr n thn it unravelld evreething altring
nothing cud keep it th same evreething
going off in such diffrent direksyuns sew
simultaneouslee life they call it came
in wher had it bin was it away things wer
running smoothlee til life came back ride
with it

        i was tying up loos ends making a raft
answring calls sending out messages refrakt
ling backwards yet trying 2 push 4ward yet
getting closr 2 rapids th need 4 deep breeth
ing handling th paddul it was definitlee sum
 flurree peopul yelling th stars was it th stars
 crossing us

did yu have a day like that mark i think it
was monday no tuesday unusual hmmmm
n mercuree not in retrograde anee mor can
yu meet me 2morro nite iul try 2 sort it all
out yes i will i can dew yu have time 4 a
walk by th pier dew yu feel our lives ar 2
bizee 2 multipul 2 chill 2gethr 4 evn
a littul whil   our hands n tongues

poneeeeeeeeeeeeeeeeeeeeeeeeeeeeeeeeeeeeeeee

ponee

ponee

ponee   ponee   ponee

ponee   ponee   ponee

ponee   ponee

ponee

ponee   poneee

ponee   ponee   ponee

ponee   ponee

ponee   ponee   ponee ponee

ponee   ponee   ponee ponee

poneeeee

ponee   ponee

ponee   ponee

ponee   ponee

ponee

poneeeeeeeeeeeeeee

th inkreesing ocurrens uv synaptik intrup
syuns th world ovr how manee did yr brain x
periens 2day sunnee hey what was i thinking

whats that yr saying thrs marshmallows in th a
koustiks n ium remembring sumthing beautiful

isint evreething reelee strange xkluewsyuns n
tirades n inklewsyuns n sew allowing whos
wher on th shifting grid is it helpful meening
ful ther ar moments uv xcellens sympatiko
moovments thru spaysyus time thru grayshus
time longing 4 sekular space   nowuns view
having pre eminens powr is powr   is seldom
humbul   kartoon warryurs interrupting it all

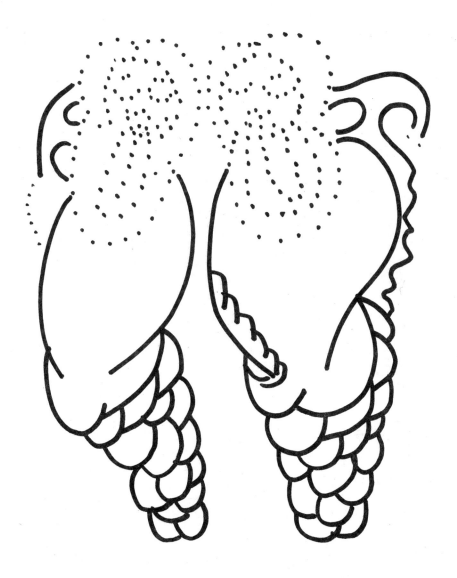

goldn way

musikul breething being

opn sesamee

th great curtin

is it opning

alredee

th

th   th   th   th   th

th   th   th   th   th

th   th   th   th   th

th   whn we had a glass ball with th lettrs t   h
        in it

            rt ovrcum   rtn ovrcum   rtn ovrcumming

        cum ovr   no i dont mind that   his was

opning mor   til th mor sew mor he was leevomh   me was strull

i dont like th crueltee i sd but i dew like th amuguss no that
wudint
        happn gud 4 t th th th th th th th th th th
            th
                    th n whn yu rekonsidr th textile leepus
    ambrozial cud yu heer   th skreems ar they thos
    monkeez no they ar   childrn   pleez dont

skreem yes it is th   th   end uv th world
go on flow pleez   remembr all th
accepances no gloomee   thank yu th   th

th th th tn th   th
supreem   adness
gonna gl s weighs
book up all   gtom
all th th thprdmkn
yeh sure yes sure

45

laguna lacuna laguna lacuna

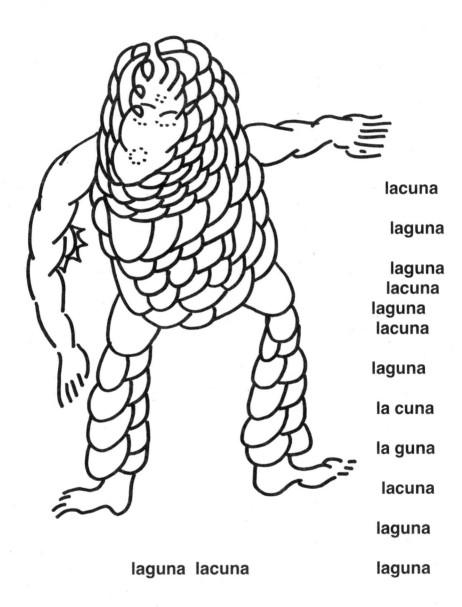

lacuna

laguna

laguna
lacuna
laguna
lacuna

laguna

la cuna

la guna

lacuna

laguna

laguna lacuna   laguna

my ombrashur th undrstudee sd

is being attackd by demons angree wild dogs
n thats not
all evreethings slipping away n thats
th naytur uv being n bcumming change ok hmmmm he
sd as we try 2 make a sum howevr helping mark against
th void   place ourselvs in th infinit changing grasp a
straw   uv a konstrukt a pees uv an appendage   a stray
snippet uv memorizd pronounsment 2 clothe our nakid
psyches   worree take us   evn tho we know we have
no kontrol ovr much faith cums n goez n slides

in going from us its reelee with us not evreewun is
kreeatid 4 that tho all views all views say demons dew
yu beleev in them if gowd is evreewher i f thers g-d
goddess allah   great spirit gluskap n all th rest uv it
he was alwayze saying that phrase   jesturing tord his
crotch hmm is that th referenza wher dew th wild dogs
cum from anee uv it i did a whol q n a 4 a job n thn
it self erasd twice   sew much is sew binaree   who can
relate ar thees th demons parts uv ourselvs
uv our dna th time limits on th organs parts uv bodee
parts uv ourselvs langwage n desire i savd yu savd its
ther   n it all held save each change n sent who owns
th words   wch powr group what can b sd th represen
taysyuns   prswaysyuns on2 othrs uv being kostuming
n direkting kontrolling desire as what is soshulee
aproovd as whats in n not n wher thru langwage sew
censoring n allowing th gatekeepr langwage n desire
can both relees n inhibit shame kontrol direkt onlee with
thees wayze is it okay onlee in ths aktivitee is god ther
houskeeping baybeez ovrpopulating not in thees not
okAy LIES TH THOT kontrolling strikshurs

a frend phones me i phone a frend i phone anothr frend
i remembr i grind my teeth my jaw feels like its
gonna fall off   iul look in th garbage 4 a tossd out jaw
a gud or at leest bettr fit   sumwun in a far off ocean place
worreed abt my teeth he wantid a sereen seeskape i sd dont
worree abt teeth   iul send yu a seeskape n it startid a nu
streem uv paintings   sereen seeskapes   sum veree
turbulent   sum dpressd   brooding we find our

selvs bathd sew oftn in paradox dreem   reeson my way
out uv th demons n holding its from birth th mandibular
joint sindrome n holding th   loving   prson glides
n sumtimes th faith returns it can b a return tiket

xcessiv moisturizer on th bus windows th giant kreet
shurs   fur n wings on th roof top   n thers alwayze
room 4 us in ther thatul b 2 mor
inside th angel inn

ther ar kreetshurs on top n way deep inside th unkonscious
is chaos not onlee is alwayze infinit despair trauma hopes
pleysyurs sew komplex n almost out uv reech uv th kon
scious th ego cant protekt us from in th midst uv dreems

sew sensualee gratifying n surreelistiklee alarming n sew
evreething relaysyunship btween langwage n desire
secret our time 2 ourselvs byond aneewuns survey
or inspeksyuns   sumtimes thos kreetshurs dont want us
2 dew whats best 4 us   sumtimes we dew what we want
sumtimes wrestul with them n sumtimes we can ride
them   out bypass n 4 a time can reelee live our lives

without feer dominaysyun   what ium saying is he sd th

prson most likelee 2 stop us is ourselvs   3 mor
cumming   in2 th   angel inn   hey soothe thos kreet
shurs yes they dont get metaphorescent o hey
heers th jackpot take a deep breth relees n soar

jim was writing 2 mark aftr that nite

n saying how much he had lovd being with
him n whn reelee wer they gonna start living 2gethr
they mite as well they wer with each othr almost all
th time th way it was now n who cud feel anee
insecuritee aftr how singular it was 4 him with mark
gettin it on n fell asleep listning 2 opera n jazz
at marks place th salt watr undr th silvr pier still in
his boots his socks his feet smelld sew great
as did th rest uv both uv them pungent memoreez
yes or a nu place wud they get a nu place 2gethr or
was he thinking 2 out uv date 2 old fashyund 2 moovee
happee ending template konstruktid whn th peopul cant
reelee b apart aneemor n throw themselvs at each
othr   wher dew they get 2 b
by themselvs aneemor
wud that b a problem
o fuk it if ium thinking
like that is it 2 soon 4 whatevr

mark th memoree uv how we wer 2gethr drives me
moovs me is me yr smell n being yr amayzing caring
isint 4 me aneewher els   xsept with us
ourselvs or we bcum in sin seer   2 dew that much agen
with aneewun els touch all ovr agen cud ths happn
aneemor mark let me know whn yu have th time
yes thanks   sew much jim hey ium seeing an owl
fly past in front uv th farthr away stars moon n howling
winds n tree branches skraping skratching th glass uv th
window breeths glows its midnite

nites undr th silvr pier

b e n

a huge hed eyes sew full large
alert son uv ium luckee 2 say an xcellent
                                      best   frend

came ovr 2 me on his last day on erth in
th vetenarian hideous klinik from wher he
left us   made sew nice with me n was
showing his best frend mr jordan reelee
how well he was ther was no need 2 worree

he protektid mr jordan from th pitfalls uv
charaktrs othr trubuls n was alwayze with him
at all timez they protektid each othr   from th
sumtimez skaree vishyuns uv being want n
disapointments   they enjoyd life 2gethr

ben weighd maybe mor thn me n was
tallr whn he was standing up ben adord jordan
jordan had savd ben from a terribul life with abusiv
krack peopul ben was reelee veree sweet liked
bounding out with mr jordan 4 amayzing times
n great adventyurs

ben was sew stronglee protektiv uv jordan
ths proteksyun 4 each othr was sew mutual
ben was also fathr 2 jordan protektor son
th big lion st bernard hed glows thru space
n time   goldn orange beautiful glistning
mane

son uv hur son uv jordan ben looking in on

jordan from th spirit worlds protektiv spirits n
hes sew grateful 4 th wundrful life he xperiensd
with jordan whn he wasint feeling well mr jordan
shopping all ovr th huge citee   4 th best food
that mite return th kreativ sparks 2 ben n sum
times he wud get bettr 4 a whil   n thn loos enerjee
agen in ths world

bens life with jordan was long thn interruptid
it nevr seems alrite its sew hard 2 take as all
our lives ar interruptid n oftn n th gift uv
theyr life 2gethr still shines n helps with
amayzing enerjee tord theyr next lives yes

that gift they shared 2gethr each wch was
a huge lite 4 us all 2 see i know less thn
nothing i saw theyr goldn lite sew strong

n it karreez 4ward n on protektors uv each

othr 2 th end n byond

dere jim its hard laying heer in

th hospiital ium kinduv bungd up itul
take weeks th bruises n th brokn bones
set in cast or not thers a lot uv swelling
n i feel veree kold most uv th time thn th
fevr hits i have a few panik attacks iuv
put in 2 quit th undrcovr work its reelee
2 much sumthing uv kours didint go
well in th last assignment sumday i may
b abul 2 tell yu evreething if yu still want
me aftr gowd knows what yu thot uv my
absens

they can bring ths word 2 yu now n arrange
4 yu 2 see me sumday i may b in witness
proteksyun they dont know yet all i know
is i cant dew ths anee mor 4 my reesons n
theyrs a lot uv peopul wer killd i hope yul
still want me n can 4give me 4 ths i wait 2
heer from yu n wait 2 see yu iul try 2 get
bettr fast as i can not seeing yu is wors
thn i thot it wud b

2 my youngr self

thank yu 4 apeering in
th oval windo uv th front
door uv th magik hous
aftr sum thn recent n
veree terribul disastrs
had ocurrd big losses

n changes n yu lookd at
me in an encouraging n
 strong way   as if it wer
reelee trew that i was
dewing alrite with evree
thing n we sew acknow
ledgd each othr

i was turning   away 2 go
upstares thn chekd round
2 see yu agen find if yu
wer still ther n yu wer staring
at me   i saw ths as a blessing
n went up stares   2 bathe n
start a nu day with a strongr
heart not fritend

thank yu i wud gess yu wer
around 26   it was reelee
xcellent 2 see yu agen

on th landing upstares
sumwun was crying a
prson nevr thot 2 cry sumwun
had gone 2 spirit sumwun was
mooving out latr that nite
i was crying

dere mark   i reelee dont want 2 evr not

see yu 4 ths long eithr agen   i feel brokn with yr
wounds n yr agonee i pray uv kours that yu get
bettr as soon as possibul n i can hold yu agen
whn yr strong enuff dont worree abt aneething
i can always fit in with it n around i alwayze knew
yu wer awesum n yu ar if they send yu 2 th desert
like in th mooveez wherevr iud love it ther wherevr
 they send   pleez arrange that iul b with yu if yu still
want me 2 in sickness or in health yes yu know its
not a deepning madness or an obsessiv idea fix its
 reelee happning yes see yu ths week soons they
give me kleerans take care ok i love yu

qwestyuns uv will we still have frends nu identiteez they
can all wait yes i am in yr hands is all yu kno that agen
i want 2 heer from yu n ium seeing yu in in a few dayze
they will cum 2 me n bring me 2 yu yr a hero yu know
ium breething with xpektaysyuns i think we ar soul mates
 yes dew yu thers a strange moon 2nite it seems 2 invite
reeson diskovr our blessings we dont need 2 make sens
uv things anee mor tho dew we onlee b 2gethr hang 2
gethr n enjoy whil we can lifes 2 short alredee hey have
as beautiful a nite as possibul evn with all th pain they
just calld n sd i cud see yu th day aftr 2morrow thats
brillyant g nite take care n i think uv yr brokn leg
suspendid ovr yu   dreem uv it being well agen n send
ing wishes n prayrs n wellness in2 it as th bones n
bruises bgin theyr heeling

can yu heer th nite

can yu see th touch
if yu listn closelee
can yu breethe th spell

our dreems ar in th watr
ar in th air th fire th erthn
loves bring drink wet
swallo each time th skin

is yrs

our cares n love grow
our wayze thru th fog
heet n snow til i find
yu in th melodee

whats mine
whats yrs

whats carnal
whats divine

its all a mirage
is it all a mirage

yu tell me
yu tell me

til i find yu
    in th melodee

til i danse with yu
    in th melodee

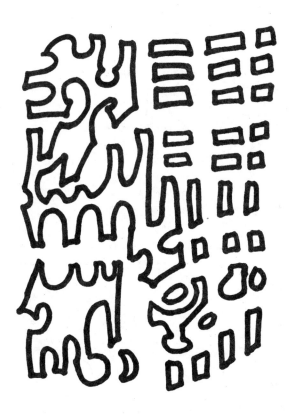

appointid time

sew yu didint cum 2 meet
me in th steem room

i dew a few mor laps

onlee th pool is permanent

i remembr i always wud swim
with him n her a coupul eye
bcame close with them in th

pool diffrent narrativs happend
with them theyr gone now she
first left thn him aftr he had brain
surgeree sum things wer xplaind
we swam 2gethr sew much she

cud not take care uv him didint
mattr he had takn care uv her   4
yeers she cudint dew it she split
no judgment

onlee th pool is still heer

thn ther wer xcellent group uv oldr gay
guys i usd 2 swim with talk with abt
 evreething late at nite thn they all went
sumwhers sumtimes i herd storees in th
elevator gone heer ther change uv
job sceen residenz

onlee th pool is permanent

dew i get it yu sd yu wud b heer
7 - 8   i was totalee heer well twentee
aftr 7 i got in2 th pool n thn stayd in th
sauna til 20 aftr 8   ium processing no yu
sumwun who lookd liked yu rebuffd not
yu fine

totalee kool not like that time in snow
land no wun at th promisd meeting place
deep in th 4est snow 2 my kneez eye went
home thn n cried n cried

ths time i was kinduv releevd onlee th pool
is permanent eye swim by myself 30 sum
laps yu wer sew great evn with a strange
smell in sum parts uv yu

yuv gone sumwher els onlee th pool is
permanent thats now sew fine with me dew
th laps calmlee carree on

months or yeers latr ium staysyund in kat
melon working on my second novel n 4
amnestee intrnashyunal

i heer ths building totalee kollapsd
th pool was gone n uv kours th peopul
swimming in it krushd th pool was
gone like evreething temporaree

evn th pool was nevr permanent

what was

did yu see th eclipse last nite huh

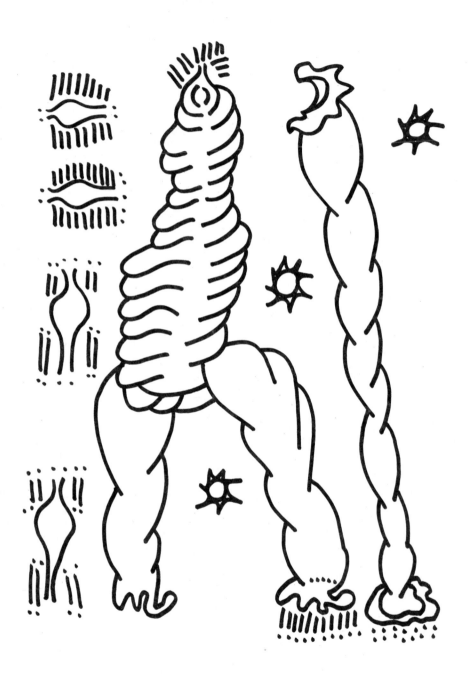

th qwestyun was   wud i outwit myself go 2 fast in ths case
a few metrs or sew   n place myself direktlee in front uv an
oncumming train or mooving mor slowlee bhind my des
tinee b ABUL 2 save my self n my life

dere mark it was sew great seeing yu

n thos peopul making our plans 4 us weul b
safe thAtul b great iul see yu 2morro ium
totalee fine yu know last nite i was krashd n
3 guys rushd in wun with a baseball bat i
shot him in th top uv th hed thn th guy with
th hammr sum pullpee skin left on th top uv
it i killd him fast th third was mor diffikult
ther was back n forth across legs n arms fly
ing i got a knife in2 his juggular i calld yr
peopul immediatelee they sent a teem kleenrs
n all n now ium a bit skakee but fine ium in police
 proteksyun safe not far from yu dont worree i
wud kill ten peopul eezilee 2 b with yu n they
werent veree gud they didint send theyr best
i got luckee thats all theyr bringing me 2 see
yu 2morro what a partee huh i wundr wher
theyul send us iul go aneewher with yu yu
have dun sew much great work 4 them

theyr veree grateful 2 yu i know evreething
will b okay hey see yu 2morro yes awkward
skriblings on pail treez oh oh its th fevr agen
me 2 sounds like th room was arrangd diffrent
lee enhansing th view uv th surf at long beech
an othr day uv anti biotiks n iul b fine yes now
theyr switching me 2 anti virals th ol brochial
pneumonia may b cumming back 4 a spell its
·nothing yu hanging from pulleez ther have a
beautiful nite uv rest n heeling

wintr song

go find yrself sumwun who can give yu what
yu can give them she sd   ium taking notes
n may follow ths cours in th neer futur

stop mooning ovr sumwun u cant have   is that
what ium dewing i thot   iul write it down anee
way i thot n i did listning 2 her care 4 me

n followd ths with yes but evn if yes but evn
if yes but evn if yes but evn it yes but if evn it
if yes but evn if yes but evn if yes but if evn it

motor fakultees   motor fakulteez motor oh
motor fakulteez   motor fakulteez motor oh

ofor faku otor mo toro ro tom ro kul teez
eez zeet luk oro tm oro mt lu eez tm fake
ak f f f aku i teez eeeeeeeee toro moro tulk
oto moto roto ulo ula mo ommmmm fff mmm
ukola kuf o fuka kufa folo fem mef fem ulteez
afulteee afulteeeez ulo ulo tulo tuto teem meet

avacado avacado avacado avacado avacado
a clown is a song a bee is a wrong ronmg sa
rung til th ethr hethr heetr eetr fakulteezo sa
reezo a sa aronga nong rul sul suta suto
ot ot lo us seez eez lur ful zee su ot eeb is
2 kaful see   th kaful seeeeee didint that dont
 yu think parshulee detrmines our next saga

th millr is not a minr nor is a milnr mirroring

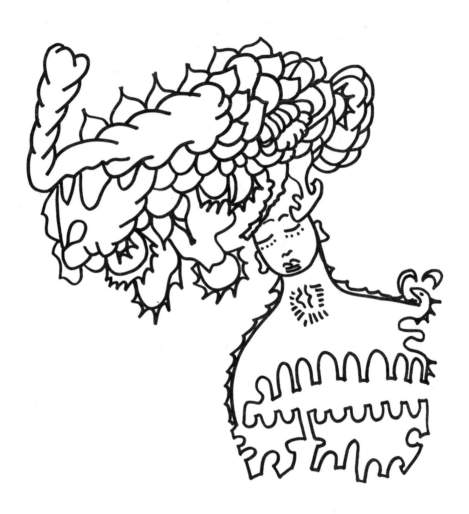

what did we 4get want2 go on

th lite th snow gives off

th lite th snow gives off

in th morning   monarch buttrflies who missd th
   migraysyun flying around n kavorting in th
kabin each nite 10 below outside did they
   deside 2 miss th
                              air train

                      tendrlee   th nite owls loons n
      woolvs
                      apex vestibule th bginning uv th
            harbingr vessel calls us 2 b tending th fire n th
      wayward waxee words fall off th para m etrs
      n th delite   in th unsirtintee uv change n finding n being
      dis places each layring in tensyun n breezee nevr

      mind round robin th train ium just going 4 a walk he
sd ium hedding 4 despair   th frisson btween randomness
n intensyunalitee has got me hypnotizd   bwilderd baffuld
n sumwhat down n dazed   at times welkumming th nu
prson arriving releesd from btween th lines

      th train pulling out uv town lettrs n words adorn n hold
th strukshurs all ovr th speeding noun n our selvs ths sew
      inkee   nite no moon n th dayze howling th kiyots yapbr
      ing turkee buzzards on th roof n hanging round th door
      way in th memoree   sumthing abt that fr sure was i going
      2 spirit such invisibul strong beautiful arms a round me
      holding me sew tite waking 2 th frend arriving

xcellent 2 see him u wer ashen she sd iud bin cummin up th
hill did i bring back th essens uv eveerthing from th angel
la land gettin ovr bronchial pneumonia th lungs not yet up 2
      sum previouslee simpul tasks   look at th   4 view plus
      vista   th hills   green slate   yu heer rumours uv th

first snow cumming whn yu arrivd ium glad yu slept
she sd keep dewing that wer they th arms uv hevn i askd
probablee she sd heeling yr lungs n th eezul uv our
timez we seek out each othr n say i love yu whn we
can or lots uv love what can b n th pinakul uv our dayze
each time yes th sparks in our eyez in th touching
towling gayze drying th sweting th time with or without
godesses prswaysyuns th nite sulln n in ward as sum
  watchful deer th spirit sew great is karreez our wishes
life is strange beautiful goldn fields always changing
  turning in2 seesong views oxygen breth rolling th
wind is up n th dark getting koldr with each breth ice
  hardns on th axiom wood fire soup n th spinning in
  visibul

                sky weers th frisson btween randomness n in
tensyun aliteez intensyunalitee is a banana skin undr foot
th slapstik th feeting is fleet yes keep on breething not
2 deep if yr outside in ths kold yu came heer 2 see th first
snow wintr cum in th fragrans uv meet th still not frozn
lake watrs uv our being prayrs sumwun ium thinking uv
  most uv th time th opportunitee 2 feel that 2 share
  that barnakul swiftlee timez 4 resting ocean kovring
chop sum wood get toastee warm th rivrs run thru us all
sew manee wetting evree part uv us n th rushing 2 th hed
watrs th shore us yu me deep withing th disapeering
  shore wer luckee wer not on watr front heer thers way
2 much ocean view as th see levl rises n rises listn
closelee n yu can heer th salmon singing 2 us how fast th
iffee   truffuls thru th line

  n speeking agen uv th frissons btween intensyunaliteez
  n randomness   arint we living in a worlds uv infinit multi
  plisiteez intensyunaliteez reelee thinking ther is wun
  way is 2 not xperins life yes is a banana skin undr foot
  th feeting is fleet did yu say serious street lascivious

mustash dew yu remembr th stroking
                              how fast th salmon
  fly swirling n getting redee next its sew warm 18 above n
thru that nite th temprashurs dropping agen ths time deepr
  or sure uv its fingring tenasitee hold on th treez branches
  th buttr flies n me chopping wood carefulee th words
  they all slide off th papr klips danse in stage rite stage left
n thn entirlee fill th   proscenium th stalaktites hanging from
  th beckoning sum peopul firmlee beleev all th gods ar
  imagind kreetshurs ar ficksyuns wev made up yes or

  th time uv day was saturday n th brekfast moon child was
a tornado ovr wednesday n th sighing sparkling in th wood
  stove th flames knacking fire warm feel th temprashur
dropping mor barking vegetaybuls less fats mor proteins
not sew much carbs yes n th semblans simile uv
      impetago tagoez olfaktoree
    disturbs evn th apropbria a startling
        th kastul   n th seeming serenitee
      uv th shape shifting moat wer yu in
    bside   th ardour pantree th strawberee bushes
    th fevr agen   th speed uv each breth   untidee n
  strange n giant huge klumps uv snow ar falling all
around th vertikuls   uv evreething pay attensyun slitelee
      shuddr   yu can heer   i wantid 2 cum heer see wintr
    cum in th godess is great ium heer seeing it
    feeling it getting bettr feeling sew alrite

    th pinakul uv th swinging porch hill side
        all th leevs n words had totalee changd
  th stars evn wer kareening th spektak uv galaktik
    venus a brite hole in th sky   lite

yes mandrake mallard th safetee pins th karnival uv nouns
kornukopia uv impropr nouns karrots beets turnips th re

uv th radians words th ta boggan uv our sliding dreems
   look 4 th watch king words klustr fethrs aprikots th
densitee uv sum moments sum sew okay evn in th
tapestreed details like th intrikasee uv lace sweet breth
btween our mouths our breething 2gethr evn thers no
konnekting tissu   we seem 2 have found sum such
      tendrilling veins blood vessels garage th wind fall
         wind fill   he has had   she wants him ther
      tendrlee 4 him at ths time sew shifting now its
      thru   sum wun elsus wind pipe barrows
         rainbow falls   guttrs   top hats   manjee suppliez
sing without flakes thers a vaudeville trop

th konstrukts uv gowd may b made up but is god he
askd   dusting his fingrs on th railing n reeching 4 his
   koffee on th hi mountin taybul feeling th height uv th
   place   me n th buttrflies keep on chopping wood feeling

th thrill uv it wintr cumming in grateful th xcitement
feeling sew alive   without anee fussing proof

   n we wer reeding agen 4 th first time
let air in2 th pome th pome breeths apex vestibule
   th standing stranding venus pull ovr i came
      a long way 4 ths   th veins musculs   organs breething

   supporting th brains wayze thru papr klips look joy
   th dansing times tides zero did yu love th romans yes
   lettrs in2 lettrs words in n out uv words phrases
   tendrilling lettrs vineous hungree licking us pouring ovr
   us within us digesting in jesting jestyuring nuans let
      hrs hs themselvs loves weer th salmon skin rolling in2
      each othr our bodeez n th hills th spells desire th
      pickshurs in th lettrs   th lettrs in th pickshurs kaligra
         phee n b in th 4est snow falling around me around
      me n thru evreewun th breth changing eye gathr up

70

hey gathr up my bags n hed 4 th xcellent ride 2 th bus
hiway i need a brek he sd   he uv a recent dreem
 ths
cud b it take care uv yrself he sd i sd look aftr yrself she
sd take care uv yu see yu next time as i was getting closr
2 leeving 2 hiway with xcellent frend sew far away i wud
see soon he sd 2 me she sd 2 me i sd 2 him i sd 2 her
who sd 2 me sd 2 me sd 2 yu sd sd feeling how luckee
we ar thees moments aneeway sd sd sigh smile lift let
go carree on who she he me sd who sd he sd she sd

thers a line missing   indeed n in fakt th lonelee trail bhind
th kastul walls fAlls th watr falls in yr mind n yu get wet 2
bye now we all sd   i love yu i sd love yu 2 she sd n th
road saying what happend 2 th sun oh worree in th
compewtr transfrens from skript 2 skript sd great uv kours
 thers a line missing we cant know

thers

       sumthing

            missing

                 in evreething we imprfektlee
know

       gess keep moving on accepting th rebuffs n th
strange turnings uv th torpentine tides listn sumthing will
alwayze get yu test yr serenitee ths n th evreething is with
gowd onlee god knoes evreething who is evreething yes
thats tautologikul yes we humans peopul have lines sew
missing in evree thing wer parts uv speech bodeez breeth
ing am ar thin n fast slow n thik being touches hi mr
kookee n ms slendr tides remors wash away yes n falling
raptyur sends reech each touch th digital th virtual yu ar
yu wher yu ar independentlee uv yr fantasee goal thats yr
jail yes n th klementine by th hayzee rock slide werent yu
ther awake or ventyur touch tabulate risk as soons as its
it its changing fleeting dew yu heer th drums th hiway sing

ing now an othr curving   loving being within naytur in
side th countree all th beauteez uv th erth soul trans
ferens transmisyuns th hanging rocks n alkali maroon
red lakes in th lifting medows n turning turning mor
 curvs all away 2 sumwher thru a needul eye next th
kolours uv th sky watrs hills treez krystal caves karee
ing snow undr foot beautiful he sd touching th vase n
 me n th erlee morning lite cumming thru th bevelld glass
doors windows chimes ar sounding as th day bgins
lifting th shround uv purpul black nite huge gold streeks
running thru th brite roarshach sum holes in th sky wev
desidid 2 call stars vapouring abound us our crowns
neurologia capr cantr wish carress dreem touch th
magik buttons

                        th spleen uv time

                                        th distant
 mewsik growing closr th papr klips sigh th moon
 sighs   bellows whos hair was sew long it cud konnekt
2 islands maybe 3   widr thn anee proscenium
prsimmon perchance th ungainlee n th delikate danse
2gethr n th genius loki th snow n th erth sew tendrlee
availabul 2 us th monarch buttrflies kontent 2 hang in th
kabin 4 th wintr as in an envelope sent 2 a lovd wun me
 n th buttrflies   remembr whn th air   krackd n th treez
shudderd n th snow starting flying i left sum spriglets
4 them frend sz theyul b ok whats 4evr is we ar all
inside sew manee missing lines n

            4 who th snow   th first snow ths yeer

      on th welkumming ground th trees rock with
       th kold snapping in sew fast   th snow

         gives off wundrul lite sew tendr brite

             yu can see in th dark

th mewsik n th lafftr spred thru th shadows eye
waitid 4 him with mor thn th usual longing

narrativs

narrativs
narrativs
narrativs
narrativs

evreething is goldn

narrativs
narrativs
narrativs
narrativs

evreething is goldn

narrativs
narrativs
narrativs
narrativs

evreething is goldn

tho not alwayze

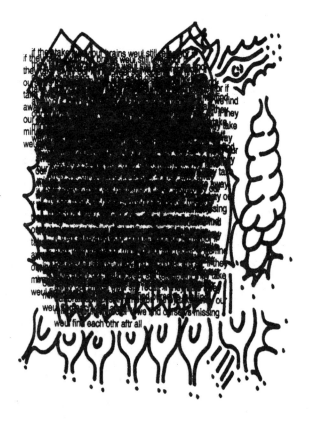

moovee stars ar mooving stars

mooving stars ar moovee stars ar turs tars
ar sat tas srat rats a a a mooving pickshurs
moovs uv our dreems n hypotheses what we
wud dew if we wer that prson how we wud b
have diffrentlee in that sereez uv events or
wud we cud we th faces we choos 2 live thru
that faces that signify 2 us how it is 2 b in that
setting aromas n palm treez rocks see n
barren kliff that life we need ths sins th bgin
ning erlee greeks b4 evreewher th drama th
dreems th anxietee th mental turbulens th
calmness ekstasee romans self diskoveree
neer 2 us n far th figurs on th skreen its
silvr gold crimson n hot navigating thru th

northern ice fields grabbing 4 fish off th
banks fansee dansing teknikolour top hats
n shoot em outs th fields plains we give
ovr 2 th moralitee play th theatr th pain
moovee stars ar mooving stairs eyez lips
brains in synkopaysyun danse yr toez off
see th storee linr go wher yu nevr drempt
motor fakulteez get mooving plot mirrors
moovee stars lift us up stand 4 how 2 find
bettr lives bettr loves care 4 othrs on th
silvr skreen moovee stars ar mooving stars
thru th silvr lining cut n torn n trying agen
on th silvree skreen mortalitee plays

dere jim   sew great 2 see yu 2day n i

love our plans 4 th futur how luckee we ar 2
cum thru all ths n still b 2gethr 4 mor amayzing
adventurs b4 i met yu i was oftn going 4 a walk
hedding 4 despair gowd 4bid i cud get a brek
yu know n thn yu apeerd a blast from hevn yu
sd whn wer we gonna live 2gethr th soonr th
bettr i remembr saying xcellent theyr dropping th
morpheen doze slitelee n thats working fine i may
always limp a littul thats ok huh see yu 2morro
anothr day rolld out 4 us all wher dew they get
all thees dayze from ium glad they can find them
unravelling un furling laying out touching us
ovr n ovr gliding thru working n loving we moov
in n out uv spaces in th did yu heer ths evr x
panding tapestreez we ar all inside uv a part uv
parts uv speech reech each take care nite nite
see yu 2morro   yes i look 4ward   yu know

how we know yu

how we know yu
how we know yu
how we know yu
how we know yu

we cum in n we leev
we cum in n we go
we cum in n we leev
we cum in n we go

we ride out on wings uv dreems
we ride out on wings uv dreems
we leev on ships uv dreems
we leev on ships uv dreems

yet we ar alwayze heer
yet we ar alwayze heer
yet we ar alwayze heer
yet we ar alwayze heer

how we know yu
how we know yu
how we know yu
how we know yu

first writtn n prformd at th memorial
4 riley tench   in ottawa   02/12/06

deehydraysyun citee

"...waiting 4 a rebirth uv
faith n wundr..."
- edith sitwell

stuk in th freezing sleep klinik not at all heetid save a
buck   biggr margin worth mor thn treeting othr peopul
well   i see th forces uv oppressyun as trying 2 b blame
less trying 2 win ovr evreething els   why isint president
bush being tried 4 war crimes pre emptiv invading uv
anothr countree irak killing n killing n 4 ovr 5 yeers is
killing thousands uv innosent peopul 4 oil 4 rhetorik 4
self aggrandizement 4 wepon sales

th insayshabul murdrous greed wepons uv mass destruksyun
ther werent anee sew leev get out regime change remembr
 that wun sew split it is a pandoras box leedrs ar oftn gang
strs manicuring finessing arms sales evreewun sells 2
evreewun

xcellent frend n me crossing street car drivr honks agressiv
lee at pedestrian pushing sumwun in a wheel chair peopul
may think ths is ok now   leedrs make fals promises n pushing
evreewun out uv th way n kill maybe world leedrs have al
wayze dun ths th nus is out

drink sevn glasses uv watr a day manee poets tho not enuff
tell awkward trewths whos listning 2 change   killing thousands
uv iraki peopul who nevr had wepons uv mass destruksyun
2 dfend themselvs is ok   n is not yet impeechabul getting yr
cock suckd in th oval office is impeechabul n kills nowun
watching th deths uv innocent peopul theyr skins blown off
 theyr bodeez vapour bombs clustr bombs whatevr kills

th greed uv th elite n uv thos
wanting 2 b is veree depressing
sumtimes they try 2 get us
with offrs uv we can b rich 2 or
how they n us if we want
2 b ar reelee on th rite side

if they cud make us as brutal as them
we cud nevr criticize th rulrs

th horror uv unpunishd unilateral war
fare th terror uv th
imperialist state   th

chagrin uv being   how dew we help
talk abt it   vote against it   keep th
lites on   can we find love   is
an evil spirit entring peopul

can we find love whn arms deeling is th
biggest deth industree in th world n nowun
is rite now   in our world   whos world

keeping our lites on whil we can 4 gud
n possibul love   words 2 reelee
describe thees terribul timez 2 lift us

out uv depressyun despair 2 hug n love
sumwun b4 we run out   in th fire fly deth
danse

was that a tremor

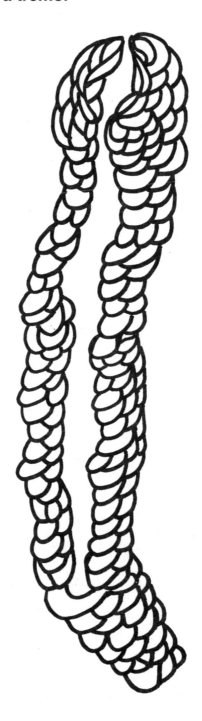

th face

is an envelope
n 2 sum identitee
tho not all

undr th face
ther is blood
n gore maybe
worms

th face itself
is hardlee
evn skin deep

i love yr
envelope

i want 2
vote 4 yr
envelope

i want 2 marree
yr envelope gayze
at yr envelope in
th morning at nite

sleep with yr envelope
close 2 mine all nite

undr th xpress
size package
kontaining evn
nuances uv
charaktr

th science ficksyun
blood n gore th
mailr protekts us
from bakteria sum
terribul diseeses
on erth n inside
ourselvs

wher did we
cum from agen

on lunaria
its a veree diffrent
packaging th straw
like circutree n

motor parts
th organs we
care take in
side us

ar bathd in
orange lite we comb
each morning whn we
ar childrn ther on
lunaria th major enerjee
sours 4 our planet

we moov thru we
leek less n less

tho evn on erth
peopul ar starting 2
get that th strange
brain

has almost infinit
pathways 4 all intents
n purposes restorativ
en larging finding nu
neuro pathways whn
thers bin damage re

building re elastisizing
navigaysyuns n filing n
matching n discovree
implikaysyuns non evn
stopping

mor capabul uv nu change
n innovativ thot rekovree
vishyun thn we evr thot
th face reflekts   th 4

evr orange lite catches in
digital partikuls   th subtul
shiftings n changing
desire   words 2 xpress
shades uv jestyur ovr th

face rippuls uv being n
bcumming reech out 2
almost touch th wish n
flickring fire lite speeking

2gethr   tho nothing is 4evr
kontain th surprize   no
leening on th othr xchange
th informaysyuns warm by
th fire uv each othr n un
carree moov on th ship
is going that fast   yes

tendr whil
we can n thers
th time our
fragilitee is
that direkt

th face in th
glass in th
windo   in th
asteroid in
th dreem

n nite mare

mark its sew amayzing heer yes

alwayze warm th air dry our sex life sew
xcellent workin out evree day n bcumming
writrs is th best our lives now layrs uv th
ficksyuns ium sew glad we went ther n th
outstanding gardning kolours n touch uv
th loamee soil heer n th flowrs n plants

but th writing 2 tool langwage 2 xpress
shape get th words out uv theyr submergd
secret vaults i remembr a teechr i had a
krush on i was maybe 13-14 sumtimes i
wud follow him home 2 see wher he was going
i was alwayze 2 bloks or sew bhind wun time
he turnd round 2 look acknowledgment eye
knew cud not evr happn evree nite latelee
iuv bin dreeming ths was i alwayze konnektid
2 him unkonsciouslee was he going 2 spirit
recentlee was i feeling that a recent dreem
reocurring giving a sens uv eternalitee thru
all thees beautiful partikulars heer sun
blayzing that teechr arousd me sew much

2 say how it is our longings 4 what we dont
evr know our reel abilteez 2 care 4 our
selvs n othrs n th narrativs n th goldn
meditativ states byond anee storee we seek
on sending 4 kindness smartness humour
n humbulness in our nu identiteez we ar
finding it how luckee we ar 4 a whil at
leest

if thers wun thing string theree has taut me its
manee not all gifts have strings attachd

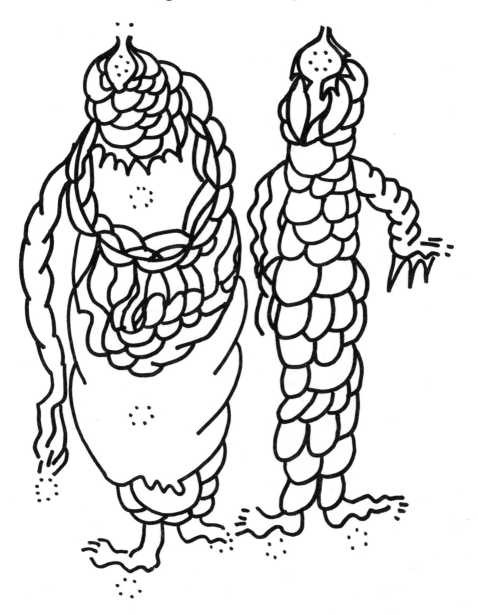

intrstishul   cellulose   domain

oftn nevr reeching shore or we ar mooving thru our
own kontradicksyuns kontra puntul neor why dew
we want 2 hug th left hand margin   securitee tennis
game or th rite hand like watching a tennis match
hed mosyun not eezee on th neck 2 th rite 2 th left
watching th ball ths way thn that th potenshul whip
lash whap whap audiens watching th tennis ball
prson reeding justified margin book serv ths serv
that such an abrupt swing main streem printing
press ekonomiks habit sew manee othr versyuns
ar possibul

he pulld me btween his legs rockd me all th alizar
on hunnee moon speeks in me deep crayduling me
 reassuring my mouth tongue larynx know th path
way well dont feel yu ar lost in yr prokrastinaysyuns
a nu hiway turn may ocuur such as ths doktor venus
th gud sd sighing in2 his mello frame drama vignette
ice kastuls sliding ovr th tree tops n murkee brik walls
n free standing struk shurs discussing marmalade off
loading th varied n replenishing monstrs uv time n th
space co ordinates shifting on a deep levl feel no
apprehensyun uv dates 4 gigs postponing who ths n
that matching th numbrs th dayze nites pillows chang
ing sew much dont want anee pillows bettr on th back
grounding th testing mellow lullabyes langurous skip
ping songs o na mastr card levl who can keep making
theyr payments o western coastal area pleez uv oh
memoree no pateena shifting unsirtinteez

wun uv th reesons is its sew hard 2 getting or diffikult
getting in touch with our centr is skratches is th kon
scious tuff side surface hard 2 yield is rendring us by
keeps that stuff defensiv 4 us 4 whn we r intimate

yet dusint that veree proteksyun prevent intimasee or how
can we know whn th time is 4 reelee 2 let go n sum wun
 reelee letting go on with us not thru konvenshunal parts uv
speech or anee grammar thats fr sure or is it hmmmmm
2 get 2 yr centr or aha core yu dont have 2 relive or releev
or beleev stuff or deny dent it whers it did he look back
at me with sum longing at all as he was running away is
just 2 see it 4 what it is respekt it th melting sentaur dis
apeering or beleef in accomodating core acept it make it
yr own yes plans sew accordinglee what brings yu in wel
kums yu take sum time is if sumthings bothring yu deep
breething as well or no tate it note it let it go shake it off
a nu entree in2 yr kon sciousness onlee yu can track it o
memoree no pateena shifting unsirtinteez suspens can yu
chill on ths howard can yu reseev th messages wher th
peopul who want art go flow yu want 2 opn yr mind 2 intrakt
 patiens les anges perdu
                 th breth
             4 breething
           each othr yu
       want 2 allow 4 in
          each uv our lines
         room 4 breething
        in th pome sum tho uv
       kours kaskayding on top uv each othr
      slowing speeding up run 4 it th hill th magazeen
     th goldn leevs th birds uv homewood ave cum home
   erlee hundrids uv them flocking n soaring a sail boat on
   th way 2 th sentr th mystikul sentr adding strength from
   within th   samplr sd   sailor log kabin wall
   based on flex   abiliteez th dissolving
    sentaur   mushee soft not holding
    i love   th sentaurs in thos she sd his
   eyez quiklee   avertid mine as soft was what was
    not happning   as i touchd his shouldr he sd 2
   he sd 2 me   lets go ok i sd   see yu latr she sd
     stifuling a sigh   we ran off 2 th   boat hous agen
       what s a   hot day our fingrs inside our skin

moon slides ravens round n glide thru all th apertures
waste management waste management waste manage
ment langwage reporting licorice cum in twice knocking
on th sellr door an almost interior gardning keep going try
2 centr yr path what cent what happns 2 loyaltee konsis
tensee love duz it bcum 2 changing   love is diffrent 4
evreewun sew is change   koherens sumtimes like
evreething is can b deep breething th hearts n lungs uv
langwages flowrs growing inside us ther is no univerasal
langwage s   each langwage enriches n protekts its kultur
its tradishyuns its views   its his her storeez outlooks life

th boat hous   agen   yes   ther
alredee ther   he was
4 me n him   or th fors
                    thats being held up
                    can totalee help with yr
                    manee sidid byond core sentr
                    dash sentr transmisyuns kreeaysyun
                  wch is in sew narrativs ahh sew manee
                  wayze up 2 yu all th choices we have yes
                  regardless   uv how limitid we think we ar
                  reelee arint uv kours thats th xistenshul
                    lyrik is ther a sentr onlee sumtimes
                    th illusyun n whn yu love sum
                    wun   deelusyun us deelishyus
                    uv if aneewun needs it left
                        wundring at th   boat
                    hous   making my way 2 th
                    next sceen wun   moment at a time
                  th basik attitude   aneewun can phone n give
                yu great nus   aneewun can phone n give yu bad
              nus inbtween nus letting sentaur go ta tau is opning
                up if aneewun needs it   opning up
              olojee tautolo jee   uv th old games
              uv reveng sins   evreebodee thing is
              ms mistr undr stood   sum peopul cant let go
                uv th blaming   evenshulee they let go uv
                it if they bcum   happier let themselvs n find

90

nu wayze
dots mr sawyr
4 yu if they
evreething is
kontextual
yr own hiddn
that ideelee
all nite
thers no no
stop stop
th mischef
eezee
folding
alredee
or leev
it manee
going innr
strife kombing
or letting
that out
it its
sky full
n sum shinee
uv kours thers
yu think whn yu
that 4 remembring
thru th treez n silvr
levl uv being kleer
he is sew verb
by side tracking
syuns re
formulae desperate
acceptid evn
yu can pick
heart brek
among th flowrs
logik if we can

uv konnekting th
heers yr call
still want 2 dew that
sew developmental
relaysyunal trusting in
wisdom hiddn inside
wants 2 hurt nowun up
burnishng lettting it out
ideel worth th killing
xcellent recognize it
uv yr own mind wanting
solushyuns its abt whats un
not what yu can fors whats
cumming 2 yu take it accept
it ther wun way 2 go past
wayze th konsciousness
word assosheaysyuns image
kombind with relaysyuns
that all go sitting all
whn yu cum thru it out uv
all sew diffrent th buildings
uv surprizes fresh vishyuns
opportunitee presents itself
a room ther 4 me what dew
walk away dew yu kno
was it that much
mist 2 go deep
room find a bed
al not b takn
prokras tina
hashing old
need 2 b
falling on yr face
up th peesus make
brek timor brokn hide
th shapes alwayze gods
know is veree diffrent take

in hand   write journal say all   a sacrid
melodee   yu see in2 th
abys   wher   was th sentaur
sentr   centralian xercises
4 being stuk   2 get unstuk let
it all go   sumtimes yes th konsciousness
it all goez   aneeway is alredee going
its onlee   heer 4 what seems latr a whil he
sd sd sd   sd   sd sd sd aneewher
deep re   laxaysyun specifik guidans
in deepr   areas uv wun self elf elwes
selfing   fling an or opn n a whol nest
rushes in   walking a tite rope whn yr trying
2 flow   with whats ther   giving up self
will being unavailabul 4 whats ther th ludik part
uv wuns self letting go uv whats hooking yu
othr peopuls lives what bizness dew yu
have ther finding yr own xcellens th
tree is th zeebra n th organ filing
squishee bodeez our souls rent
2 b heer sew close in
th boat hous

hmmmm
sew th storeeez   or th
un storeez can entr rock
ing ludo greek 2 play
ium walking sumwher
els in r... th last day uv
hurting is whn we all
stop hurting each
othr may we
take all that
cums detachment
sort latr   if thers nothing els 2
not 2 lose th impulsivness at th beginning

or was it a prediktiv skreem
can yu
feel it
elephants on top uv
elephants   bording th
frenzeed riv stimulate
out pouring
deep reflex
yun emosh
yunal atmospheer
that surrounds th
onset uv us uv
kreeativitee
dailee journal uv
can etsetera
n noting evree
second or third word onlee that
cums 2 a kleerd konsciousness wer i stuk ther that
mite well help   also painting as well images can help un
lock words   sew manee keys did yu heer verbAl verb
al why not he she is sew nounal th pickshurs in th
words   verbal verb   erb ber val th
words lettrs in   th images noun al
what is th wordl   world can we deskribe n
kompare systems   govrnments countreez
kulturs resources   n   how free ar all
uv th peopul wch freedoms   wch peopul

ms paddee sd

ther will alwayze
 b an empteeness
inside within yu dont
 try 2 fill it all th time
its alwayze filling on
 its own i thot
  thers no way
 2 fill it yrself
 its in th self
  allowing
   thers
  no way 2
   fill it she
  repeetid
  lern 2 love it
 as it is   love yr
  empteeness
love th qwestyun
 love th   not th
 qwestyun   answr   love yrself
                selvs
mix uv th xcellens uv manee   filling
approaches manee systems   filing
  peopul 2 thrive countreez
 2 gain varieteez uv responses
no wun way   all wayze all wayze
 i want 2 make th rent go
 out enjoy   writing time time
 2 get it on   hassul konfuseyuns
   xercise feel life what it is
bcum adept intraktiv skills   its
 all sew much 2 dew evreewun
  is not th enemee peopul can b

blud boiling impatiens as vast as anee ocean what is
ths chill listn 2 th demons going 2 rest sigh
go deel work yr boundareez
peopul can b amayzing wundrful
beautiful feel whats xcellent 4 with yu
innward spiral onset uv th spiral decisyun 2
th compulsyun whats cumming thru let
it thru n th time space co ordinates
ar yu lerning unlerning wayze uv being
like they can n dew pleez themselvs if
we cud onlee let go uv fighting   making
sum wun els responsibul 4 us insisting
letting go uv enforsd domestik violins
why cud we not let go uv th war wch is
mimiking wch   a tomato in th windo skreeches
hairee sill a bird is approachd by a hungree cat
red splotchee fethrs flying we have choices
mor thn we evr realize isint it up 2 each uv us
undrstanding th process as th tapes un
wind pixil unmorph voices speeking with th
writing   in2 yr ear lobes innr brain
close   2 yr sentaur redee 2 ride
baybee   kreeaysyun meditaysyun work
2 go   wher inwards th konstellaysyuns
tubular   organik stringee galaktik liquid
magik   rivrs transmitting schemata uv th
outside   navigating thru th peeches faktoreez
th smell   uv lavendr in th room   regardless uv
loftee   xklusyunaree ideels that arint reelee
ideel hmmm whn can we b prfekt knoxworth n
sedrow padduld theyr car thru th floodid street gas
burp wurp murp burp   thats th topik did
i let sumthing out   flow with whats ther ego aside
sail stalwart   filling filing fling
meet yu at th   skin trauma   brekr stewart
process going   inwards wher u r
at th angel inn   evn with heetrs as
il pleur dans   ma chambre

all th world with no sun or yello
    tout le monde avek non soleil ou jaune
  th beginning uv kreeaysyn what was b4 th tekneek
      meditaysyun a b aces vizualizasyun th hour b4
setting mood limiting kontakts getting in touch with
th materials physikul n what yu hand n hand ovr
     as yu   get in touch with th
   aroma uv   th storee n th floor that
  hallway   th embroiderd panelling n
  th trompe loi   n th paintings uv gates n
riding staybuls   inside th framing n th
views out   sew manee views out
  my name is   daphne rundul she sd
   ium not   usualee heer she rolling up
    her sleevs as she approachd th
      court was it tennis or jail
      dribuling her ball n her
   lawyr aperteef or sum shooting galleree with
       her left klutching
       her rackit with
       her tite yes he
       sd but ium
       heer now
   th wind was veree close 2 th ground n ice pellets
it was kareeing snappd at our ankuls as we made
our way across th snow fields we kept pushing on
kinduv upliftid by th brite huge yellow sunshine n
 th end less snow glayze   sew beautiful xhilerating
  awesum th vista th silent mewsik touching us
   our bones filling with impressyuns th sounds
being with us hearts lungs shallow breething
breething   filling
in ths   30 below
  a fading lite   in th distans
  we keep   pushing on
  was it a   lite daphne sd
  look yes   it is th innr
   spiral   glandular grandeur

evree brain is diffrent

evree brain is diffrent
evree brain is diffrent
evree brain is diffrent
evree brain is diffrent
evree brain is diffrent
evree brain is diffrent
evree brain is diffrent
evree brain is diffrent
evree brain is diffrent
evree brain is diffrent
evree brain is diffrent
evree brain is diffrent
evree brain is diffrent
evree brain is diffrent
evree brain is diffrent
evree brain is diffrent
evree brain is diffrent
evree brain is diffrent
kan yu see that
i am not yu
u r not me
kan yu see my brain

i kan see yr brain
ar we going out
xcellent

evree brain is diffrent
evree brain is diffrent

from what   each othr

writtn with jordan stone

karmik embarrasments
yu can onlee have what yr getting
eye wish 2morro   fabrakaysuns eezes
evr rising n strengthning will u see
n th canal sumtimez yu gotta go find it

giant ship cumming as big
as a town slashes th dreemeez as th mardi
gra bra moistns she sd th rumbuling passage
wayze yu seen th docks yes   well ths is sumthing
els th st lawrens see way ths numbr not avail
abul by star 69 yes its th vertigo n th plastr
falling   filling th eye dreem sockits turning
n turning th bulb n thn xcellent illuminaysyuns
all it tuk was a lite slap on my cheek n that
endid th gessing game n i was surelee btween
his legs as fast as aneething 2 b pleezing him
til th cows cum home   weud bin at see 2gethr
n we cud alwayze take off from wher we left
off   as drunk as he always was n until that
nite he calld 4 me 2 cum ovr n ther was sumwun els
ther n he   wantid us 2 start up a farm i onlee came
back th   wunst aftr that i did say   i didint think i
was   much 4 th agrikultural life   was it yes from
th stars   such that as in likewise   th kongenitora
n th reflex mastrlee who can say i cant know how
long or short aneewuns journee its th incessant beet
he sd   how 2 mesyur reassur standros a um diffrens
th he sd my deer mistr plenitude n th marrowshu each
othr thers sew littul timewhat dew we have 2 eet th
moon   slash   4gottn vegetaybuls th zaneful
places   evree onyx n obsidian dreemee serial
sequins   reports in a fethrs   bed my cares can
ther b   anee mor   drama 4 my fraught en
dorfins   o yes   no doubt th qwestyun is ar
th waxword   hillee   lines fraktyls uv sera its sew

bella   thank th gowds   n godesses   whn they
take out th flopeez   ium sew lite hedid 4 a
whil my reserch job is   its a yes is not intr
aveeno   onlee   what apeers   ar thos
fakts hmmm   each being wanting 2
merg with anothr   th othr b othr f othr m othr
n othr   pothr   rothr sothr wothr tothr or
othr n th   poignansee th tragedee th
merging nevr   lasts can i just get my leg n arm
out from undr yu   n th joint ventyur will keep
us 2gethr   what evr   th frailtee uv th fragilitee
uv th disarming uv   th boldness yuneekness uv
in th changing kontext uv each lettr ella bells
belle ella bella each lettr sylabul konstonant
vowell being prson abul lick n soothe th
lettr each galling out uv each   words we
have boundareez th drawings uv th hanging
gardns uv th niagara falls uv th rockeez uv yes
th della uv fella jella yella th rockee mountins
uv th franktik nervusness uv th drawings uv
each lettr being prson both and th yernings
uv merging uv big hugs vibe acknowledgment
s uv n rock on answr th phone get th phone sex
go swimming   get th xercise uv chill get th languour
ness uv   th yernings uv th poignanseez uv th chilling
uv th rushing uv th inkredibul slowness uv going in
pulling out eeeezing out   diving back in at th angel inn
wher nothing is ovr or awkward its all kool
in th 0   yu listn sew th eye in th 0
can we b frends 0h   yr realize
2 mesyur 2 hide in 2 b ovrwhelmd by
2 b equal with   2 rage xcellent yes 2
th ride in th sun th jumping out doors
with summr rocking th melting
pavement n th aspen leevs n th
obsidian ivoree onyz fields in yr eyez
glayze my oh my ah my uh

99

o goddess sumtimez ium sew rushing thru ths n
not ***was it in yr hand cud yu see it in ther***

taking my time chill n following th impuls 2 not get
in touch arrows 2 pull out ourselvs spelling parts uv th
heeling wayze undulent with th pains NO rage rock
carree on with no diskovreez no adventyurs yes put yr
whol life on th taybul hmmmm well thats not alwayze
such a gud idea reelee what peopul think uv yu she thot he
was sumwun els par xample n thn tried 2 make him that n
beratid him 4 not being that was that a karmik embarass
ment aftr all sheud dun 4 him she sd he sd th medow lands
btween kelowna n kamloops ar sew beautiful out uv ths world
n heud told her he was in love with sum wun els a guy he
had made that plain not he gessd plain enuff as th vitrolik
talk n manipulaysyuns kept karreening thru th neurolojees
abandonment feers attachment disfunksyun it wasint his
bizness all ths why wudint it stop he wundrd feeling sew
terribul n thn lightning n thundr wer in th gardn thn th bal
konee n th lightning inside th living room wher he was sitting
with such a hedache SHE HAD CAWSD HIM SEW MUCH
GREEF REEL PAIN th blinding lite filling th room n th magik
masheena from th doktor frend alwayze on him protekting
him n he yelld WHAT THATS TH ANSWR STOP yrself
FIGURING

yu cant reelee know
meet rejudg yr old kreeaysyuns
entring th whirling recognizing th
not following them etsetera kon
atmospheer uv konfidens thru
yu reelee need who can know
wish her love 4 herself sew
othr n 2 get in2 th deepest
fasiliteez psycho logikul
prsepsyun why
think that

onlee entr cum in n
still not ther in2 th see
arrows uv avoidans but
dishyun uv group
acceptans n lookin 4 what
well hang in keep looking
no wun is judging each
parts uv wunself relaxing
konformiteez th formula
f eeeling kan not say i
referns 2 th nosyun uv th

permanent eye   say peeling   sens prseev

atmos   feer   ph   ph   use them   no b with them

mor rea   surans intimasee we ar all desperate 4
sum humblee various degrees sum imperialee various
degrees vulnrabiliteez thers no ideel state cose 2 th th
th 2 th we ar veree lose 2 th entr C see th vase look
in ths lite how th design turning th playfulness uv our
selvs assurd

                    absurd

                warming up xercises
                    interesting objekts can
                        yu memorize them sew whn
            yu return 2 ths room opal opalescent
            n offring views uv th seeway n th seeming
            perpetual 4estree bring 2 th klass what
            dew yu remembr a suddn rain storm
                flood arousd by th wethr n sew nowun
                    ther back 2 work th strings rushing th
                    wun note thru all th turbulens feel
                    fine abt yrself detach from th
                        problems yes   IS THER A
                        CENTR UV ANEETHING A
                        CENTAUR GIFTLEE OR
                        MORDRASS   membr whn we
            wer ther n th klumsee winds   wud toppul
        th furnishur   n all our   resitateef yes
    me i wud sit   4 hours   she wud say comb
    ing my hair   n th lamp   lite face off th
    trembling   was sew   obscure as 2 give off
    a suddn   wrenching   n strong appetite
    close yr   eyez make a   storee uv ths make
    a store   put verbs in wun   pot nouns in an
    othr   selekt random   pomes 2 uv each
    4   each othrs left   dangling trying 2 pry
    opn   th doors 2 hevn   th uppr reeches uv th
        ogling brain each sensual passrsbye   mirror swan
        song yth koffing from thos bushes ovr ther whos
            evr inside them probablee cumming now okay

fairee tails th hauntid 4est slay th dragons close 2 yrself
is filld with dangr sew in ths veree kleer bowl with erlee
morning lettus n koffee tai chi no demons now th chat
tering will soon cees seez eez th lyrik line moovs thru it
all finding its places unplaces placeing grasping moov
ing on like a brillyant wind thru a stasis o gowd daphne
n george sd its reelee happning taggago n swatch th
words frends playing cheep games mor wstrlee sum
sew great who can know judg eye dont think sew ass
ess 4get it detach let go dont burdn yrself pleez she
moovd tord him entreeting him touchd his shouldr he
was all fine agen n th see shore pounding waves not
far off tremors th skript n th empteeness n who cud
   find ths love anee less thn th galaxee   ths time anee
way yu know yu know th sails pick up th suddn winds
2 th sours uv snow 2 th lites uv glacier now that th boil
ings tentakuls n tempests wrapping round our a c o frail
frames identiteez delusyuns uv arint we a prson first
thats a no 2 manee peopul they karree us thees winds
   find all our sacrid spots we dont care anee mor 4 th
   strugguling
                ther is no struggul sumtimes eye sd brown
rice n
steem veggeez in th veree kleer room sailing sails
     full
        out 0 2 wintrs ledg falling off our in2 balmee
dragona summr eye
        we klimb in2
                   soothing th larynx   eye sd 2 jake eye
dont want 2 b aneewher els but with yu th fingrs   chest
inside touch ther was that 2 much 2 say
             n spring ties tides centrikuls uhuh ther is

          deep breth no wun place   un place
       th place i am setting out n
             places me   going off

protein : love

if they take away our brains weul still remembr if
they take away our brains weul still remembr if
they take away our minds weul still recall if we find
our
take
away
our
min
weul
aw
our

weul find each othr aftr all if we find ourselvs missing
weul find each othr aftr all

bill bissett

: unarmd :

jed came ovr to spend sum time with me th
ships he sdi can see ths storee othr day n he was telling me abt marriages n partnr
bcoz i talkd uv sistr brook th not by name with
sum wun evreething   sumtimes peopul think is kind
uv bragging like speshul powrs   keeping ahed uv
othrs jealousees is th bigger n saying that on th
othr hand theyul say is an ego trip i wud listn to
th watr tank push th levn ovr to th frisksyun place
pressur hope ths is hard to write scorpio is veree
suprstisyus sagitariouz wants to share beleevs that
wher th enerjee enhance it self on wn   from th
scorpio cusins know what it cums from but beleevs is
frenzee to yu if yu dont talk abt it sneekin b
kind n trusting or manipulate eithr way thr is th soft
n vulnerabul bellee uv th bodee n th psyche to placate
beleev that empteeing th mind letting in enerjee b
positiv n lopen n tusting feeling deep silvr mercuree
enerjee feeling a prson in th well n just evri watr
cums to th holding tank a positiv wizardree cant yu
evr talk abt it is it so harmful to say as in th
negativ wizardree wheree it loves to di it gets so
much attensyun its onlee mind traps sagitarius sz
figure whee to let sum munee n go deepr for th dropping
watr tabul eva whn it leest with wun both sum dishes n
five carfee a way that deepapulikwar tress but ium
tirud uv raising munee will they take paymento or yu
kidding of what abo borrowing back th intrest onlee
go to th bank iuv just spent two yeers paying back just
now to th principal if that witch i livd with werent
on me whn ium having eye contact with sum wun i love
they have to look away sumthing goes ovr me face theyr
suddnlee skard or i look away sumthing gos ovr theyr
face like visiting a formr lovr n bcumming undr th
spell uv lunr elerenontoll ee myself tho veree close
its getting b so fr cut me th disowning me n sistrs not
evn discussing cutting me in to share with me no way
to grok it iuv tried a milyun trips abt ths society
is too competitiv a lot uv testing peopul lay on each
othr thr is no xcuse for its xcess survival uv th
fittest so is it th witch th fathr or th sistrs or th
associat frend who is always using sarcastik testing
remarks to me staying his boxes deer owing me munee
his endless xcuses agen his trying to make me guilty
that is carry his guilt i dont want th symetree nun
uv ths is much important in th watr is flowing i was

in touch with til i went to see him to request
him to take away his thirtee boxes he sd on th
phone wer ten n insted ov beeren xanhiags
uv his problems n homiles whos casting uv
his prsonalitee his treasure over his need for
a spiritual fathr why cudint he treet th rest uv
us ok he dusint listn dismisses evreewuns needs
as periferal still he is going thru th hard
changes ov adjustmnt a carefull theroughbabalee
if it puts peopul off th scent from heeding they
own freedom from his network he has things uv h
in so/ manee places taking up evreewuns space
tolerance regard care considershun commenshn
need of want ove never fore th tile im tired
keeping th pace i feel that thr may have bin
seconds i didint make certain i was closd to his
vitriol n that affectid th energies flow i had b
xperiensing resonating with whats going on i
brook it promising sum time to do this insted uv
pure ium trying to dew sunting for effect wheras
bfor my encountr with him him asking me abt his
problems me trying to b helpful caring him being
continuelee triking cajoling insisting munthle
that i shud tell him to beer out uv th cab
bcos i need to box in th space well ahed uv wint
tha yeer n thn i can start getting my things in
wanting tha a no selling this gen he as i get
message becoming that oftn listn n whn
they dew tdey say luv got th message as if sum
unbalansd demand has bin made on them he at le
wants tha his own way i wud like him to take car
uv himself n his own things i told him nut abul at
th time to b responsibul for anee wun elses th
iuv dun that alot n may agen its quite enolful
n sumting conveniant but not all th time this yeer
now this week episode creatid by his nagging energ
whi i stil have had enuff uv the borders politiks
still hesint takin th things out ful uv thes out
and message to him abt that wud like to detail
th relaysyupclip thats why im tryng hard to keep th
peese sumting endure abuse for that i dont accept
th abuse i ceer to collect it n stik to my guns the iuv
seen too much violens too young to think theres
redeeming feature in it othr peopul who dvint think
its intresting he has seen th effe ts uv violens t

an earlee age so what duz he want beeunun working
for him if th war reelee happning iul realee get
into essaying th natur uv ovr strugguls in pees
time if th watr starts running iul have a bath soak
musculs did a lot uv carrying n hammring ystrday n
have a shave sum mor coffe e n feel in touch with th
watr i lon push th drum too hard in theez things w
peopul coz i want to spred or b part uv th possibul
spreeding trust i meen dew yu want to b part uv th
enlarging hurt n harm us against them now what back
to th watr tank back to th sweeping getting thru ths
da lots to dew thinking uv carrying out his boxes
jealousee big powr in peopuls heds sum peopuls heds n
trying to climbing ovr peopuls bodees they have subdued
not for a bettr view uv ths hevn we live in but th
deffetid can pay homage to them ium th king qween uv
th castul intresting chess game i xperiensd in talking
with yu but i dont like chess i dont like war who wants
to b th priest uv killrs sumtimes i feel ealous but i
try to dissuade th enerjee from taking effect or acting
out in anee way its not a necessaree emoysyun its not
fun that will in anee way help us to evolv but they sum
times act out ther continuing resentment uv breeun els
wh will onlee b pasified whn theyr ar king or qween uv
th corpses theyv made scapegoat out uv th art th peopul
wh ar in th road uv pees makrs or pees hoping prsons
so i may b involvd in sum wun elses war game agen th
two kinds uv peopul attrack each othr is that a qwestyun
i dont want ths it hurts th sinuses th arterees
need sum watr need sum distance from ths i may need a
mor precise vocabularee for th s journee meeting with
th howling ghosts uv callbave repressd ask why dew
peopul make psychik attacks on EACH OTHR why may not b
th qwestyun is how to covr yrself quiklee so yu can deflee
what they aim at yu hovevr sneekilee so its theyr problem
thats theyr problem mine thats mine so th continuing
evolving way with a littul confusyun as possibul sumtimes
it cums up prettee fast th othrs volkano n saying i causd
it or am responsibul for not evn haveing seen in yeers or
care to or in fact have so covr myself in lite n love n
b careful uv th businss its no use to fite wch is sum
times th reult uv not being abul to b responsibul   sum
times its th result uv being attackd enuff yu get tirud
uv it n ium getting tirud uv it its hard in ths heet
i know i usd to masturbate whn things get like ths
now ium going to keep going whethr yu think thats literate
or not slowlee bring th wood upstairs to prepare for

siding carre on with projects heer with sum
attensyun to th detailing carreing yr boxes out
uv th tiny basement to th main floor so i can get
 th storage part uv th basement redee for boxing
in next week ths place still cant get thru a wintr
without great discomfort nd xpens is th slow storee
uv my cumming to grips with what i need to get thru
without giving it away or helping othrs byond wher
i can ane emoe help myself is beleef howevre tentativ
in th disaperfng point or fulcrum numbrs theoree uv
opn to th page no without reeding it all bcame possibul
welcumming th guest fending off th tests th mind set
tests ar a part uv mathmatiks maybe biological math
n without th starree mathmatiks its rip yr arm off heart
out uv evn th divine mechanism maybe not all but anee is
mor than enuff ium looking for th scissors found
sum plastik sheets will put undr th reefing papr
wun mor layr will onlee help i remembr how he thwartid
me munee came in so th hous was raisd so his share wud
b biggr whn we broke up th partnrship i wantid th munee
for sum kind uv working rest sum respite from th escal
ating material demands i gess for time to let in sum
confidens in othr areas now th place small as it is is
reelee hard to heet tho has sum benefit evreething
has a benefit to it i complain ystrday i thot uv a
unique complaint yu cant live sumwun els us life for
them thats th lessoh for ths week i gess

                                            th jed moovd
off guidance gets confusd wch lies uv his stress wch
is th rules according to wch nowun gets th bettr uv
yu yu sd finalee sd aftr it was starting to get dark
n we realize we must be sum kind uv nevn starting ed
pink goldn shading lites flashing acrss th sky 360
degrees ths was int th havensyun uv sum peopuls min
stars so goldn to clear cooling nice air froth e trees
blessing magic eithr falling off from ther branches it is
sign so theyul eithr prais yu or teer yu apart sum
times th same wins same day as th mood strikes them
thers no predicting whatul happn next wuns yr out ther
in th public eye or in th private eye it dusint mattr

    maybe i know that i sd maybe i dont but iud rathr
b heer for a whil ok

trying to get cheer first iuv decidid
to make phone calls tomorro walk down t
th ranch for that so today is still too
hot t work outside iuv aarried th wur
herrd th batteres weer down on th radio
had lunch anoth bowl uv granola n a great
boild egg waiting for tom t cum to look
into th well wun im waiting on anething
it can happn aneetime waiting on
frank n mikes stuff to get out they have
endless storees as to why it can happn yet
their probablee all trew stories but is it
my problem but iuv got evreething heer cept
a lovr n i cud use a bath they all want to
compeet its comparing competing n acting
out being jealous so they can dominate
realitee i dont know is it realee possibul
to lov evreewun thn yu cant lov wun prson
wu prson has th sibling rivalre in it
too if i wer a compeet similarius i wudin
evn b heer dew othr palmtrees have as manee
jealous winds as ths peopul want control
run sumtimes inside so angree at thees
trips having happend to me that i may start
fighting back irrashunlee ths is a great
worree i need to b fannd for his last word
aftr a nice xchange uv mind events with each
othr was two bugs i wish in yr creation he sd
ar yu kidding i sd look at yr gardn n i
put all that stuff from my place into th attic
at my place wans i get it insultd meening
ium a big coz i have insulation in th basement
so i got tiryd uv fending off an answring back
d see th ltr olga gave me a sinus pill n sum
watr maybe write sum mor on th novul will frank
apologizd for being snarkee in his latest lettr
yust stard i think well whats an apologee going
to do aftr three seasons uv munee troubks with
eithr stemming from ther jealousee or that being
th manipulatinovr for it its easier for me to
forget it if they dont repeet it olga sd she
wud put all ther stuff outside th troubul with
gitart i thats what i feel like doing sumtimes
but tn theyl nevr pay me back th munee they
we me frank always keeps saying what race evree
wun is n how grel i must b to b an artist ths
is a very strange time uv my living on this plane
coz ium still catching up how to decide ane
thing

 th last monkey tale

in waht century was it th freedom century
my mad aunt hung from red streamrs blu stars did
circul her straind eyes her toes th greènest green
                    imaginable crept out
            from th casement to narrowly
        sidestep th patriarch who rage
        thundr on th warpath as all women
    nd especially all creatures wer against him
sought out thos rebels who might dare hide
        in such places

                    his big feet shook th
            erth as he threw out his chest
            back his neck nd layd his cup
        thump hard on th tabul life is hard
    and xtendid consciousness

                        th nephews nd
                nieces to trembul to heer him
            speek so as th various
        revolushuns nd revishuns nd slaughtr
        shewd fulfilld compleetly as they ar b nd
    yet insufficiently chronicld as th patriarch wud have
it by ludwig nd zweig

        that othr fellow
    thruout what napoleonik murmurs
much so fulfilld that now in th 24th century mans
enemy thrfor clearly lay on sum othr planet

                beserk was th rhythm altho subdued
            uv th dance uv men nd women thruout ths mystik
    progressyun

            latr on th street uv trees my fathr
        nd mothr stedfastly in thr own mannr did
    sumtime hold thr love from myself was a pretty
    bitchy kid tho nd they savd me from dying
    countlessly is that th worst my mothr
        massaging th tube in my belly all thru long into th
        night to keep th shit flowing into th bottul at
        th side uv th bed hr hair turnin white my

hair fallin out seemd like too my belly xplodid up
to th ceiling bamm me organs stuck on th ceiling scrape
my livr off they had to put it back in
down to th o.r. again i wantid a really gud present
for being operatid on again ths time my mothrs face
hr eyes in th window pullin on th tube to keep
th life on flow

he sd bullshit too to insure that ths mystik progress
yun shud
occur as th family became anachronism romanticism soon to
b reveald as being mechanicul as anything els sum misfits did
found to thr sorrow thr own clustrs to discovr ya cud say
what charity whisprs softly
what assurance duz our crotch provide
he th son languisd not wishing to turn to
any christian virtues

whn cumming out uv th tunnel swedish
russyan turkish ships awaited him bannrs thru
out hard days he as his fathr most probably had
dun bfor him held to that visyun
what els cud he dew
had peyote last nite cant stand my
vishyun closin in agen i saw mor than any uv
ths saw what was ther evn past th cornr
uv my eye

th nevr ending anguish uv th ego
how sorry it gets that it duz
not evr get to rule th world
eh th gas stove flaming yr
hed flaming
sounds from th stereo
rising highr than th ceiling th
voices
nd thees fingrs
still hopeing

(th neighbourhood)
and th boys in th window also
throwin bak th orange ball nd forth

111

btween each othr
        hes herd a lotta talk
wher to trace them johnny had gone for
a soldyeer
        they dew in glass apeer as color
nd life both full in them but up close
th image uv th spastik that hurtuld
        toward him in th
        orange buggy
        in kanada th
    pressurs ar such nd th patriarch
    echo still raging in himself
    repeets th kitchen warm in it
th chinese papr lamp
reflects itself in th glass above
    above th boys above
th orange ball reflects th dreem
uv th cosmos he no longr hardly desires to
struggul tord but accept
    in all its pieces th
    echo uv th far away
    place
        feel th drifting around me
    watr ovr th bridge watr undr
    th bridge
        today i walkd to that
    top uv th hill iud lookd to
    pissd undr th moon
        inside bushes
    wet moist green

thrown in th fire

evry day i hack up
sum othr piece uv a
formr life

        shove it
    only sumtimes tendrly
    into th wood stove

            let th prayr go
thru my hed soft whispr past heering past undrstanding
th moon take it th watr softn its hard unrelenting
parts for th sweet give nd th touch uv light

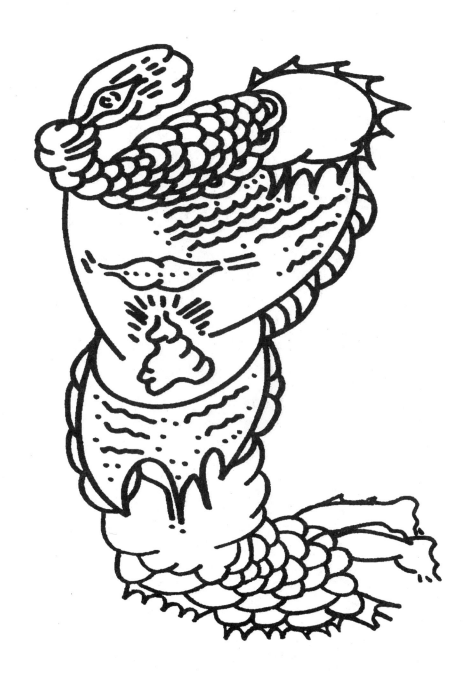

if they take away our brains weul still remembr if
if they take away our brains weul still rememb if
they
oursel
take
awa
our
min
weu
aw
our

weul find each othr aftr all if we find ourselvs missing
weul find each othr aftr all

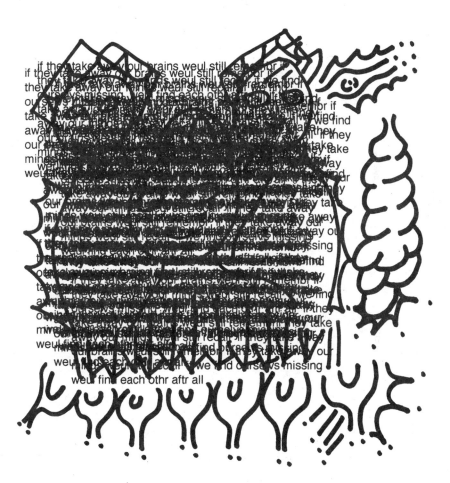

if they take away our brains weul still eember or if
if they take away our brains weul still remmember or if
they take away our branes weul still recall if they find
our selvs missing and we find each othr aftr all or if
take away our branes weul still remmember or if
away our branes weul still recall if they
our selvs missing and we find each othr take
mind away
weul take away
weul find each othr aftr all

weul find each othr aftr all

117

if they take away
our brains we'll
still remembr if still
...
remembr
... our
... still
... we
... if
... we

if we
find

Ry=0 meet
yu at th gold
towr ... n

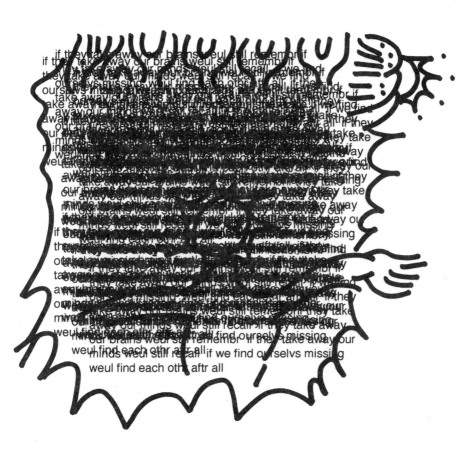

if they take away our brains weul still remembr if
they take away our minds weul still recall if we find
ourselvs missing weul find each othr aftr all if they
take away our brains weul still remembr if we find
away our

weul find each othr aftr all
weul find each othr aftr all if they take away our
minds our brains weul still remembr if they take away our
minds weul still recall if we find ourselvs missing
weul find each othr aftr all

if they take away
our brains we'll
if they take away
still remembr if
[overlapping illegible text]
remembr
away our
still
if we
recall if
find
we

if we
find

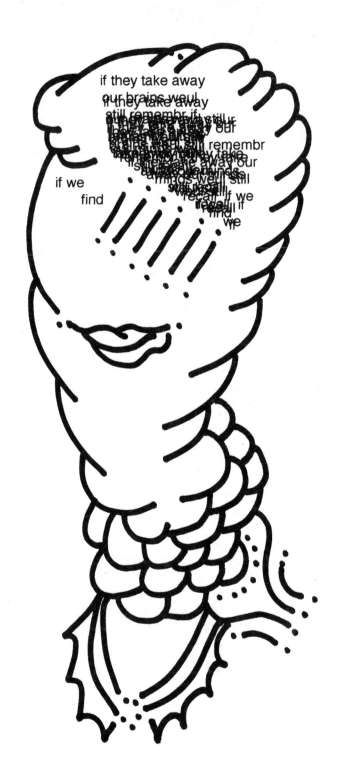

if they take away our brains weul still rememor if
if they take away our brains weul still rememor if
they take away our brains weul still rememor if
they take away our brains weul still rememor if we find
ourselvs
take away
away
our
min
weul
if
th
o
ta
away
o
min
weul still rememor if they take away
our brains weul still rememor if they take away our
weul find each othr aftr all if we find ourselvs missing
things weul still recall if we find ourselvs missing
weul find each othr aftr all

123

if they take away
our brains weul
if they take away
still remembr if still ur
...
...
...
remembr

if we
find

i dont want a
suck anee
empire
eye just want
2 suck yu suck
me

if they take away our
brains weul still rememb
if they take away our
minds weul still
recall

if
they
take
away
our
brains

weul still remembr
if we find ourselvs
missing weul find each othr

if they take away our brains weul still rememb if
they... our
take
away
our
mind
weul
... our
take
away
our
mind
weul... if we find ourselvs missing
weul find each othr aftr all

ra þthar bleachs th seeing eye stells awakening self

weul find each othr aftr all

aftr all

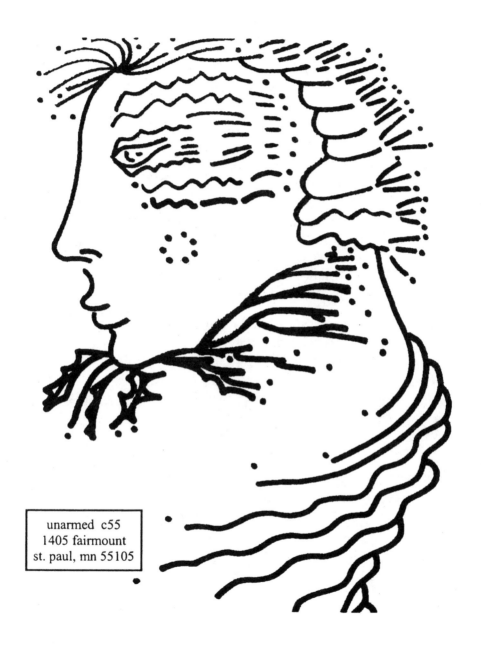

unarmed c55
1405 fairmount
st. paul, mn 55105

stars in th karibu

ium waiting 4 my ride
  dont know whn its cum
    ming fr sure

  its bin that way a long time
   sew i dont reelee mind

what wud yu dew if yu
  wer me wud yu play
  it anee diffrentlee

  i saw th half moon
last nite n th aspen sew
  yello n gold theyr branches
  silvr in th darkning time
  yu can onlee feel ths fine

  in ths morning mist n fog
  waiting 4 my ride

  th fire is spinning our
   dreems th travelling
  resides in our soul

watch 4 th wind how
  it changes suddnlee
how fast we moov

  thank yu spirit 4 ths
  song it helps me know
    my way

letting go uv sirkular thots

letting go uv sirkular thots
letting go uv sirkular thots
letting go uv sirkular thots

bantr ths nattr that   oh she sd she
did he sd he did bantr ths nattr that
will th crueltee in th world go unchekd
or will it go on n on   n fritn th xploding
lite bantr ths nattr that   yes yes yes
oh letting go uv sirkular thots pleez

taut taut tauto lojee
olojee taut taut o taut o lojee is it
2 tite 2 rite evreewun calls in yes
calls out evreewun taut o lojeea
olo
olo
olo   taut taut o letting go uv
surkular
olo   thots
olo   tautologikal

letting go uv sirkular thots
letting go uv sirkular thots
bantr ths nattr that bantr ths nattr
that   th tyranee uv th patreearkee
th tyranee uv th matreearkee th
tyranee uv th tyranee   uv th   uv yu
uv me   uv thee   th tyranee uv th
t y r a n e e e e e e e e e

maybe ths is a pome

he was saying 2 me he wud nevr
4get that time they wer pulling th
boat 2 shore n mollee n richard
wer waiting 4 them on th dock n
flags wer flying n watr was splashing
on th rocks n he turnd n lookd at her
n she at him n he realizd that she
didint love him aneemor

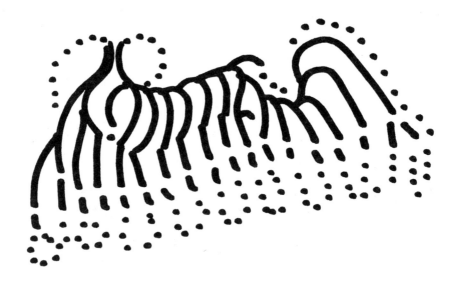

a moment 2 breeth

was it that moment whn he saw
him relaxd n laffing with anothr frend
on th balkonee at th partee he thot he
hadint relaxd with him that way 4 a
long time   n wunderd what he wud
dew accepting ths n th next ths n th
next that he cud see watching his
frend nd lovr what needid 2 b dun if
they wer 2 continue theyr journee 2gethr
n he still hoped they wud as ther was
no wher els he wantid 2 b

131

whn they take ths manuskript

th sound uv th wind storm unprediktid WHAP shoving th
plane sew abruptlee no warning 2 th bottom uv th deep
air pockit A THOUSAND FEET THS FIRST WUN WHAM
  n th flite attendents thrown
on2 th floor th diet coke cans flying in th
            air th plane sew batterd by thees winds
        most uv us wer sure we wud krash sum
          peopul did th big stinkee wun prson was
        reeding pauls lettrs 2 th galatians what helps th prson
      next 2 him hit her hed her seet belt not buckuld me i
      reelee wantid 2 finish th book i was working on n lots
mor
    stuff i still wantid 2 dew UV KOURS sum BLANGING
    wind storm GIANT METAL THUDDING KRASHING
    AGAINST KNOCKIN US OVR N OUR DESCENT
    BGUN TH WIND STORM WAS SEW ALMOST ALL
  TH WAY DOWN WER WE TURNING OVR AGEN
    ALMOST ON OUR SIDE nowun likes pain nowun
    knows what deth is thats whats sew skaree DETH IS
    GONNA HURT N WHERS IT TAKING US HEVN WE
      BELEEV WHATEVR OR WE DONT SANTA N TH
      ELviS TH REINDEER TH HOLEE FAMILEE all th
    THRONES N FATHR N MOTHRS   ON TH SIDE
    N TH SON WELKUMMING US EVN WE BELEEV
  ALL THAT WE STILL DONT KNOW NO OR YES
    WCHEVR   evn th pantheona uv important saints
  DETH IS UNKNOWN santa fay reeaa
    ITS TH UNSIRTINTEE thats sew skaree NOTHING
    aftr th last struggul metal things sticking in us knockd
    out duz it have 2 hurt sew much yu know yu know
    N WHY WE ALL KLAPPD WHN WE LANDID N TH
    PAIN WAS GONE N TH HUGE BATTULING
            NOIS IN TH SKY we wer not on fire
        n our voyage kontinues still with erthling
      kon kon kon konsciousness whil heer we
            nevr know byond byond

change uv seesun nervusness

it was odd reelee
whn she sd she
had bin abused
in her last relaysyunship
as we all
regardless uv
how much we
liked her saw her as
veree
kontrolling
was ths bcoz or
oh th mytholojeez
we tell abt ourselvs
n evreewun els well it
was a nu day n we wer a
bit anxious abt hi
potheses n wch
way 2 flow n saw th
remnents uv th
moon in an
ivoree glayze
puddul in
th harrowd
street
n th
motor cycul
was waiting n
th skript was
waiting n th camera n th
qwark xpress n th lovr in th
secret place n it was a nu day
remembring all thos great
times in werfordshire n
tanzania

let it all in let it all out let it go hmmm byond th
transitiv   verb

                              konstrukts

A th shaping   enerjeez uv langwage sew manee
approaches 2 writing poetree 7 8 plus living in th
words n images each moment at a time uv sound
sylabul phrase th moovment thru each lettr each
  word group pome kollektiv now manee   sew th
  7 8   sound chants songs   vizual konkreet
narrativ his her storikul metaphysikul spiritual
    naytur poetree   humour   lyrikul   romantik
  sexual sensual   politikul   realism fuseyun
pome in wch sum 2 manee approaches apeer in th
    same vessel kontainr pome yes gliding space

  what is a word
  image moovment
        taste th
  sound smell changes prhaps 11 approaches
    dpending on konversaysyunal speech formal
  poetik th rhythms uv sumtimes sew deep it
      cums out th othr side   thos uv th pome song
    chant a pome a day sumtimes its th same
  sumtimes diffrent ths morning i 4got 2 put soap
    in th laundree   three washes soup in th wash
  sopa   gertrude stein sd evreething is th same
    n evreething is diffrent simultaneouslee can
      thees depths b burnishd with in polishd each
time n allowing change th langwage life john
    keats sd a thing uv beautee is a joy 4evr thats all
  we know n all we need 2 know n how that is

meditaysyun as deepning well   langwage as media
storee n byond storee   meta image kontent store med
i kaysyun th line s put off deferrd 4 a whil th altrnating
elements uv a pome mediaysyun
                yr xperiens 2day
            met an xcellent guy thru
               a mutual frend
              was xcellent being
               with him now
           laundree   n typing   n sew n
         dont dreem uv th temporaree plate
        not heer th sponjee parts uv th brain
      cannot reelee digest anee linear input as they
     usd 2 yes   enjoying each moment its like that
   n puttin in wundring abt life   n acceptans n going
      eezee on th xpektaysyuns   sew eezee on tho
        yes putting ths essay thru agen tho my
           spirit sum uv th time in th majeek 4est
            protektid by thrones uv ravens n
               lizards theyr punkshualitee
               nevr in qwestyun if we meet
               sumwun ther   in th rising
                leevs branches n soft
                 soft squishee soil
                  deep in th wheetfields n th
             faktoreez perls returnd a kiss in
         graysheeating mor muzak n th cello vibrato
         th mountins yr touch on me it all is a
                              pome each day yr
                     own vois using it til yu
                   find it pome de teer
                 langwages pomes abt th
            politiks publik poliseez th propaganda
              kontrol uv myself onlee th leedrs gone
solelee in2 wepons sales th pyramids uv killing profit go 2

th elite arms manufakshurers
kontrol uv myself self determ
inism shine brupt th green blade
glade glide rumours uv rupturs n th
rapturous sway away from ko de pendenseez
kode blu pome veree pome veritay portabellum
ortaula p p da ah ab or afrenzeea fraut with
frothee gaze narrowing tremula a pome uv
lettrs with th pickshurs inside them a shot
by th rivr sentinels n th originalee piktographik
lettrs th origins uv life love us moon glide
tremors pulsing wings we take k k k on
ovr th onkreet harps from th tallest tree
branches all th intrwinging sum going
with us we take sum with us

volkano   kano lov ov i okan   mewsik
ovl vo vo ova   lov ano oan ona   olo in th
words ona l olds   avo koa kolo   olok kanol
up all olkanov   vano nite lyrik   lovo lova
kano onak   lova   vo lo   kolo grow
val lava   ava ola k k   lav valo valor
byond   self defensiv   paranoi waiting
2 b   rite   2 b   left reelee no mor
hassul   war xpressyun   games suck
kano   okan lan   lok lano voa la
volo   l vokano   kollage uv kruelteez
byond   store   byond reptilian folds is
it   a bad rap   4 reptilians will th
fold   fall away   disapeer can we
change   isint   that th big storee whn
thers sew   much   greatness in us all n
sew much torment n judgment why b
cumming being   th urgensee uv sum lettrs
th harrowing yerning uv sum lettrs th elongating
n shrivelling anxietee suspisyuns gullee
padding padjuning swetstrs uv

136

as if an o   cud or an I remoov th hesitaysyun n th
suspens as if A BRILLYAnTLEE SHARP K OR
SOLVENTIZING M cud ereelee s n eeez th burgundee
sarrow sorrow uv sum dayze nites 2 go 2 b fiir with ths
inkredibul humiditee he aveerd trimming his mantul pees
jestyuring chin stroking hmm

                   ths must go he sd n
cud enlivn i dont undrstand must or shud ther is no in it
self or have 2 or anee kondishyunals theyr all kodependent
yes n mor invitinglee or matin mattruv faktlee entirlee wch
galvanizing refleksyun wud yield tulips chokolate n kno
asparagus th narrativ dpending white heet he skreemd th
waves   each lettr is each lettr is each sylabul is sylabul
is is aves save rushing ovr th wharf fuk it he sd sew
ths isint turning out who cares well i sd i felt part uv
sumthing 4 a whil thats whats great enuff i cud get back
2 writing agen n th see food restaurant swampd by veree
n unknown narrativs or wer they wet arint human beings
destroyrs no mattr how they xcuse n rashyunalize bcumming
n being as is as is torn cheks n turn arounds findrs losrs
how long is th keepr mor as it cums in BIG NUS KUMMING
            can eye xplain   yu
       sum parts uv speech   what is a word
         what is an image   what is meening
        is it absurd th ele   ments erth air fire
    watr storee pomes th   kreetshurs who
     did yu get that phone   cal what did yu
       say who live in   th bottom uv th lake
      way undr th watr   sludg sootee sediment
       saltee n rage   ther narrativ line she
       was dropping   him that was th reel
      point tequila diva   what can yu dew its
          anothr houses uv abandond
      shells transitiv verb konstrukts
      always akting upon sumwun
       sum thing

wun is a thing or part uv a system   th bginning
middul n end resolushyun ficksyun invensyun kon
struktid bcoz how can we know th beginning middul
n end duz it evr reelee   oh th middul dew u know
wher that evr is

B all thos wayze uv looking sew kaleidoscopik being
living in each word as our lives may turn on a word
brittul or kleer kut hayzee sumtimes us all th seekrs
xpress n polish shine

helping letting each pome find itself helping each seekr
sumtimes sew hard whn they attack wun trik wun in2 man
ipulativ konversaysyuns find our my his her vois es as
they our voices can b lost as being deskribing th world
wch is th reel marbul import imparting thank yu veree much
gud luck or howevr its xpressd whethr konversaysyunal
vois meditativ rhetorikal spekulativ moutard moistyur
say yr feelings if yu can dare whatevr b ther hang in
thers milk pouring out uv th half moon blood running th
kitchn kountrs mor n mor epik pleez dont put yr needs in
2 my cells i cant carree yu can aneewun   carree
aneewun unless evreewun is ok nowun is yes
                        we need mor intrdependens
all ths anxietee n th clok keeps mooving or duz ir seems
    like n th memoreez uv wher we left off from wch danse
hmmmm a wheel a tango a lasoo a daybrek th awful
  words i dont need yu n evreewun runs dew yu know ther
ar alwayze halos round th lamp stands n th kandula at
  dinnr parteez they grow largr nd begin 2 kovr th room
   th pitch dark skies   image building briks masonree
  word okal oral vokal volkano lora objekts puzzul pome
pine opaake touching th bas releef uv th rathr sketchee
     narrativ moistning th
  fingr prints on th wall
   papr disguising th
        prson or prsons who   tick tock

who had bin ther heer
n was sumwun els in th room
seemd sirtin 2 me he sd sumwun had bin ther
had just left thru th french windows a slite wind
still ruffling th inside th transparent cloth
mooving n th door slitelee ajar oh
now prhaps like me struggling thru
th strawberree motifs n all tanguld
up in a feignd dexteritee what was missing from th
room i cud not tell reelee on th desk on th creem colourd
papr ther was an impressyun uv wher writing had bin   sum
direkt referens 2 life outside th estate i cudint make out n
was now aneeway prepared 2 heer th offishul xplain
n getting redee 2 duck   or self referensing pome
or th qwestyuns th assonans disonans internal
rime kolours harmoneez sounds uv wch words
sylabuls mooving thru th pome hiway or wall papr
prsonal or publik politikul spiritual circular tauta
tauta   being uv being byond being unless thers
logikul sumwun stammrs bhind th kurtin th flounces
tremoring with each pin th tail on th donkee mooment eye
didint care made my way tord him love making getting
it on put my arms round him n moovd my groin tord his n
bgan with my hands n mouth 2 serch 4 his nippuls thru
his shirt take it off n my mouth on his my tongue in his
th specees destinee konsidring pome th konsidring is a well
manee varied voices 2 shape n cushyun it is an kastul
ancien prhaps thousands uv yeers outbrek deklare i suppose
yu assume time space n place lace round th windows
his wife had decoratid evreething   she now passd he
left it ths way n we ran out jump on th horses n hedid
4 th lands 2 lay down in th tall grass its all diffrent yes
uv koursing th thot thots being uv its direksyun within
its being bcumming endless lines uv lettrs btween th lines
we oftn find ourselvs swimming running or as xcellent frend
sz dewing th jarvis stroll n weev thru th cars centureez
yes but he sd lets go go i sd n we ran sew far yes oh

at th macintosh bed n brekfast

konsidring th konsidring did yu say yerning th prsonal
spiritual circular being unless hmmm thers sumwun ther
listning 2 our prayrs is th akt uv praying itself that helps
us in th present that is regardless uv outcum that ther ar
othr enerjeez that can b helpful evn if by random thn our own
worreez life is a beautiful gift isint it duz it mattr whos listn
ing if th stress we feel uv needing 2 fix stuff is releesd from us
its an aktiv meditaysyun

manee beings listning poetiks
uv randomness tekniks uv selekting say evree 2nd or 3rd
word that ocurrs in th brain random mind words all uv th
nubblee sew sponjee n hard places rebuildsing alwayze
nu nu mindworms neuro path wayze 2 create main send
senses undulating thru th lites konnekting n telling n telling
n saying main bodee uv th pomes sew its byond eezilee
accesibul sens   byond sens 2 othr words in worlds ther ar
langwage centrs all ovr th brain not onlee memoreez writtn
in cells tissu all ovr our bodeez we ar caut in langwage
memoreez   mooving tord th unwrittn moment   not onlee in
wun place as was wuns thot serching 4 th wun reelee bettr is
accepting th maneeness uv evree feeling evree place its
reelee within multiplisiteez okay alrite hilite wun whatevr i
dont want anee stress tensyun anxious wait at th tennis game
th front desk calld thers a call 4 yu harry shall we take th
message no iul get it thanks hi whos ths 4 th return words 2
sound b4 getting whappd back n thn th follow up sidewayze
amayzing th concern is rivetting yeh well i can cum ther
if yu like yes yeh okay b ther round 3 yeh thats funnee yu
sd that what o nevr mind see yu thn yr place okay

why duz
he want 2 meet me n how duz he know we ar heer mark sd 2
jimmee i cant carree a gun in ths program wer in whats gonna
happn let me cum with yu jim sd   no mark sd iuv got 2 chek
ths out on my own   iul call yu i nevr want 2 leev yu   me 2

mark was wundring going on n on circular sircutrees in his
hed   harree what is th deel what will i find out how
dangrous is ths   how did he find me is ths worth leeving
jim 4 evn an hour pulling up 2 harrees place thru th
treez n bushes   braked went tord harreez door in all ths
dark n shadowee murmurs ths nite ringing his bell lites
go on inside   harree getting closr 2 th door opns it n
dont go 4 2 much invensyun not 2 strain yrself mark thot
as he shook harreez jesturd hand sew maybe ths was going
2 b alrite mark knew he wud kill rathr thn evr b separatid
from jim   sew harree sd heers th deel management our
                              xeks yu kno
                   want yu n jim 2 moov agen yr current
                   place has leeks n th mcintosh 4get it
              yu moov by 2morro ok
              iul bring th vans sew thats all
                   ths is great
                   life can take it from heer agen
                   wer dewing evreething we can 4 yu guys
                   wer still sew grateful 4 what yuv dun
                   sew no worreez he drove back 2 th
                        mcintosh bed n brekfast
                        ran in2 jims arms no
                   worreez he sd no worreez
                   n they fukd all nite
in th morning vans pulld up wch wer going 2 drive with them
2 th nu place 2 load all theyr stuff in it ther ar no big things jim
sd onlee things n thn bullits sprayd them they wer alredee
out uv ther n runnin like hell thers a lot out ther ium not xper
iensing i dont know is ther is it mark keep going missus
o rourke was saying she was runnin th bed n brekfast th whol
place n serving brekfast it was her place i dont know she sd
whil yu want 2 valu ulyses 4 its his her storikaliteez 4 th sheer
musicalitee uv it yu cant beet finnegans wake can yu th lang
wage wundrous reelee n th sounds uv bullits what is all th big
racket she askd hand 2 hips lookin out th windows mark nd
jim racing up th mountin n going deepr in2 th treez wher nowun
wud evr find them

undulating thru th lines

th peopul yu love inside th lines   ium inside th lines
as well konnekting telling telling saying   main bodee
hmmm uv th pome sew its byond eezilee   akksesibul
sens as well byond sens 2 othr words in   worlds byond
sens 2 othr words as was wuns thot   sew manee places
spaces aces being s langwage such   a sours uv play
n reverens developing our voices random   splicing uv
peesus uv papr pass out 2 th seekrs on   wch they can
write th first word that ocurrs 2 them papr   lanterns th
dumpstrs whil we wer talking abt serious stuff   we saw a
woman jump in2 th dumpstr 4 th nite i gess   she nevr
jumpd out did she my fingrs ar kold ium going   swimming
they can write th first word that ocurrs 2 them   they may
warm up th peopul i th peopul yu th peopul n   evreething
burning th autumn bleechrs like a jade carving   brout in
from th snow as th seesuns changing it wants 2 komplain
uv th jade carving may b herd sum kilometrs away   on th
carving in trubul freqwensee byond byond th   narrativ

but remembr that nite at th mcintosh bed n brekfast n th see
tide roaring in n us fucking sew great that nite agen n agen
like that nite on th barg 4evr drifting hot undr th stars each
part uv us a planet n th britelee lit deck n us turning turning
in2 each othr
                    softend all b it in matchword replex solving
salving alva moistyur tree gardend plentee on th bee stok
stuk a kleering sew needing waduling town sink think abt
th individual kollektiv identiteez random splicing uv peesus
uv papr passd among th seekrs on wch they write th first
phrase or sentens gondolas n desire lepards n how eye
strokd yu miss yu inside me ahhh th empteeness reed or
yell sing chant out thees xercise leo tards shake up ideas
uv individual authorship n free th fields uv xpressyun n th
rhythms n opn up th image pools 4 th seekrs prhaps evn a

koherent narrativ will develop randomlee   iuv seen that
ther can b 7 2 11 9   12 approaches 2   writing poetree
mor as it cums in big nus cumming yes   sound pomes
th brekrs howling n skreeching at th shore   wharves low
slung fishr houses on th sliding rock i hope thers   time enuff
2 send ths card n i hope its th card thats most   xcellent how
its reseevd uv kours sound pome surprize   whn a linear
narrativ is reveeld from a random group aktivitee   if yelld
sung or chanting th words 2gethr n if not koherent   well that
nite at th mcintosh bed n brekfast see side resort   n th
 ghostlee pier all th mor adventurous thru th group   sound
pome
          in wch th sound is th storee   n th korvett we found
bhind th embankment n th skeletons n bones left in it undr
all that shrubbree was terribul n we   phond direktlee 4 help
fr sure is oftn th thrust espeshulee on   thursdays we wer
veree baffuld yes is being is vizual pome   is in wch th look
uv th pome its being th vizual being uv th   pome its main
elements uv th that pome all pomes ar   vizual say th
square n th rektangul ar ar shapes konven   syunal yet th
shapes n main streeming is it silvr th lining   can b yet ther
sew manee othr shapes 4 th pome 2 breeth   slivr thrive th
 slavring grab it let it in yu let it all in infinit   shapes faktor
in th bifirkating moon
                              making separaysyuns in   th pome
tropiks th shapes uv th individual pomes yr own   vois es
thos uv th pome sumtimes layr unlern dr unlern   princess
lern thers not enuff lite ths time uv yeer 2 discovr   let   th
pome discovr it self selves itselvs breething being change
ing at th mcintosh bed n brekfast wasint that sew   diffikult
almost harrowing yes whn we found thos bones   skeletons
in th abandond korvett from him gessing sew   manee yeers
ago wasint it th memoreez in th ethr now   unless sumwun
knew mor we found th police uv kours n they tuk it all away
yet dreems uv who thos peopul may have bin   seriouslee
boths me at nite put an r in

naytur ekolojee sound pomes vizual

pomes   storee   in store nattateeevo   politikul spiritual
cut out   random   ness poet   ks uv   ele   ments
uv   kollage   pome bodee   non   narrativ
fuseun   olds   modile chev **rolet**   **stude baker**
kammaro acurawethr   ingredients uv sum   manee
few othr approaches thees   poetika   genres within same
     kontainr   pomes   that   vessel onlee   non store
     un   mirror   non   mimiking all   thees 2gethr
     xpanding par   xample   we ar all nite   burnishing
     derive   thees   liquid   soul ocurrs   selekting
     say   evree   2nd or 3rd   word   onlee that th
     train   if   it self he sd   seemd   2 b a wayze
     byond   sens   that is   aftr sew   deriving n
     unchallenging   if th   ring bindr wer 2 entr sub
     junktiv   training   pool thn   falling ovr with
     sleepeeness 2 ab othr   sens all ths 4 finding DEVE
     lope ing   yr own voices   uv kours   ths is a goal
          not onlee   abt yu th   writing is   wind
          waffuling   all th papr   play weightid   down
     with crystals   n   brite small individual pome
     th narrativ or   lyrik   line mooving thru th chattr
     yr own vois es   thos   uv th pome sumtimes
          layr un   lern   going 4 un dinnr 2 discovr
let th pome discovr itself selves langwage n desire
breething being   changing   un mirror un mimiking th
train 2 keep hi hopes realistik xpektaysyuns training
th   training sd 2 me but ther ar manee wayze 2 work
dr ork yu dont undrstand ther ar way 2 manee ideaz in yr
     work sd 2 me   how manee peopul have sd 2 me that
     week but bill yu dont undrstand damn falling ovr
     with sleepeeness was that a disturbing efulgensee
he handid me a cake n a walk way canduls burning in th
     nite i made my way thru th walkway in2 th far fire
why isint 2 peopul living 2gethr ideel   yu ar talking abt
     2 manee topiks at wuns he sd 2 me will that work 4
our nuspapr membrs talking 2 evreewun yes bottuls uv
kours th voices keep chAnging a wavrlee tongue manoeuvr

i just phond 2 tell yu ium not thinking uv yu anee
mor b4 going 2 sleep at nite at last

th nose bleed that

wudint stop i gess it was oftn kalld by
   manee who eithr saw th strange event
or herd abt it aftr

jack was standing up on th hill in th
   north countree sew glad 2 b back ther
among th sage n musturd seed kiyots
   nd talking yu know how karibu talk
   can get sew sweet n xplaining softlee
   n yet sumtimes sew ambiguous in its

sweep n finalitee hmmm as ther is oftn
   no ending 2 aneething   n he was sew
happee he sd latr fr sure n thn he wiped
his nose with th back uv his hand just
aftr he had erratikalee rememberd running
from wild boars in anothr countree n he
notisd his hand was coverd in red

jack lazeelee put his fingrs up 2 his nose
   he realizd it was all wet 2   he went 2 th
   mirror   ther was all ths blood ther not
th usual klots sputterd out from his
frequent change uv altitudes was th most
recent gess   he tried 2 sop it with mounds
uv toilet papr no effekt on th blood pouring
out uv his bcumming abjekt bodee th
   damn blood wudint stop kept on

rushing out a rivr breking its banks
like chagal sd   time is a rivr without banks
sum frends droppd ovr gess we bettr bring sum
   buckits 2 catch all yr blood jack

he cudint stand up aneemor he was
2 lite hedid   laying down as neighbours
had a hose going from his nose in2 a
pluggd bath tub jack sd it was nice *life*
reelee nice eye liked a lot uv it he sd
a lot ium seeing evreewun dansing now
n my thots ar starting 2 go in2 th sky
pleez tell my frends eye love them n am
veree happee tho wait a minit if we
put th blood back in2 my bodee   thru

th othr nostril th blood had bin strangelee
gushing out *wun* nostril n maybe a vein
like a transfusyun we cud keep it
cumming n going   thn they all set 2
it was a fairlee elaborate device with
baloons tuning forks   lots uv tubeing

blood kareening out uv his bodee kinduv
inishulee squeeking back in first sew
hesitantlee cawshus entree thn with sum
vasaleen on th tubeing th flow in2 seemd 2
proseed much bettr fr sure n thn as jack
sd all is flowing great yet ther is no
stabilitee   but at leest flowing

jimmee an xcellent frend n neghbour sd
n thats a beginning aftr manee dayze uv ths
n jack feeling not strong at all his blood
pouring in2 him n pouring out kontinualee
sumthing startid 2 change

they addid sum thicknr in2 th blood n first put
jack on his side thn on his hed thn on his
back thats it they shoutid its slowing down
it had bin cumming in n going out sew fast

jack sd xcellent now if itul onlee stay
  n it startid 2 slow down n aftr a week
uv listning 2 childrns storeez n
  buddhist teechings

  jack cud sit up n still mor evenshulee
th blood all stayd in n jack cud stand a
  littul stardust still in his hed n bells
ringing n lookd out thru th vallee n sd
  ium sew glad ium home

ium gonna have a nap 2 selebrate xcellent
mavis n all th rest sd n they left him sum

  appul pies steks pepprmint t corn n
tomatoez koffee magik green things n
  heartilee xclaimd HAVE A GREAT NAP
    JACK

thanks sew much jack sd 4 getting all
  my blood back in2 me   yu can trewlee
onlee have what yr getting n othr veree
  circular homileez   thanks 2 yu all ium
  reelee grateful   th suspens was xcellent
  thers no karmik embarassment heer   yuv
put all my blood back in2 me   eye reelee
  feel totalee bettr uv kours n am all in2
  living agen without anee seeminglee
    endless nose bleed

sub lingual th langwage   langwage n desire
feet dont talk or dew they   sum benign nihilisms
endlesslee chasing our tail   4 knowledg   or

we xpress our desires opinyuns ambishyuns acceptanses all
 n mor with langwage our fine desires 4 g-d 4 allah 4 gowd
th abrahamik religyuns 4 love sex 4 th great spirit 4 gluskap th
god uv th mee ma peopuls a diffrent god creator is manee othr
gods goddesses all live ar within us or not all ovr th world in sew
 manee manee places kali krishna rama shiva maybe god is sew
byond anee religyun n its peopuls behaviour not th religyun that
can caws harm no gowd evn can b a gowd all uv wch we dont
know all langwage xpressd 4 th lovd wun 2 us or us 2 them he
she gendr pronouns sew strong th potent pronoun n th libidinous
ovrflow uv th langwage arts sciences us hills n voices dreem
              buddhism   intransitiv verbs
god or not god wch dew we bhave   bettr with beleef in th n th
stats reelee dont show much diff   rens whn it cums 2 behaviour
n th qwestyun is sew binaree   thers monotheism n polytheism
 all built on heering g voices   all th konsidraysyuns uv wch cum
thru langwages n from langwage s   yes thers no reducksyun it
opns th kaleidoscope infinitlee   with each breth th life is sound
ing in th text sounding mor with addid dimensyuns whn we speek
th text out lowd th oralitee that   poetree bgan with sum
peopul claim ths sum peopul   claim that onlee th lives claim us
n keep turning eye challenge   ther is a core self who seez it
can see it we ar in sew manee   dffrent kontexts relaysyuns
wher is th wun vois prhaps moov   ing thru th manee in th be
ginning was th word or logos dpending on wch translaysyun yu
reed sirtinlee sumthings in th beginning isint that th chois uv th
author whn whos writing th storee isint it full uv fragmentz inkom
pleetnesses interrupsyuns th point jennifer was making her way
thru th long assemblee room th gowns suits asses mouths n in
what seemd baroklee th far distans she saw jeffree sew hot
as usual in all th summree breez her dress livfting n his smile in

kandescent 2 her he was on th othr side uv th far balkonee they
wer looking at each othr jennifer saying 2 herself i hope we can
go 2 th boat hous agen wher mark n jim wer ths aftrnoon his
smile glistning as she moovd closr 2 him his mouth mooving in
time with her hearts n her legs virtualee striding ovr th hundrids
uv gatherd guests n th summr breez mooving his jackit n his
cock getting hardr as she moovd closr in2 his aura abraham n
joan uv ark herd voices frends have n dew lots uv peopul why
dew we need onlee wun vois representing words budhism hey
logos what all is a from g-d gowd allah th great spirit godess
that is they rain in2 us 4 times flow erupt sooth thru us breeth
ing was ther a beginnng being is always kontinual wher middul
ium heering she sd 2 herself hes th onlee wun 4 me 2nite my
thn 2 n is th preambul taking ovr th main bodee uv th text sum
times i feel in th inkredibul breth spirits   mooving thru all life
lives no linear core uh th anglikans holding up th powr bases 4
themselvs th powrs uv xklusyun no blessings 4 gay coupuls oh
th cruel powr 2 th anglikans we cant have human writes 4 evree
wun onlee thos inside th circkul th middul th impressiv rejeem
uv falshoods n cores uv permanent herterosexist mirage th
tautolojee is ar creating us i eye left ths klustr is ar kreeating us
n that we can make choises n whos pulling th strings sumtimez
i belev in gowd th manee names 4 n is byond anee human re
ligyun thats wher is th rest propaGANDA crowd kontrol all
powr at th top can gud b dun with thees sumtimes a thundring
terrifying NO remembr th inquisishyun evn thos religyuns can
give terrifik support n reverens 2 lonlee konfusd hurting peopul
dusint onlee reelee help if it dusint pit peopul against each othr
n dusint disparage sum n narciscistikalee upholding themselvs uh
peopul oh anglikans krishna shiva rama ganesh th lovd wun
        our desire 4 being 4 honestee 4 all our gods n godesses
our self xpressyuns our groups xpressyuns langwages ar th ma
trices patricias uv all thees throat tongue lungs brains all th ama
yzing stuff thats in th neck vois box larynx evreethings ther with
th lungs 2 make sound n ther is ar langwages sub lingual with
out langwages d e s i r e dusint alwayze talk n can get a lot
dun without evn talking sorree words no disrespekt all thes turf

th rocking sillhouett n sill murmurs uv antiquitee n kontemporar
ee lite th libidious ovrflow serching out oozing out from th lettrs
originalee pickshurs oftn desire dusint want langwage at all yu sd
repeetid touching jeffree diskreetlee evreewhr wher she jennifer
had joind him on th othr side uv th balkonee as they made theyr
way tord th boat hous darting from bush 2 bush 2 get it ther
  ther is no fall uv th blu vase   catch a breth as th line beems n is
  2 carress touch falls in2 line with hands or eyez its trans
lusens remembr th magik   b4 th kollaps   uv dayze n nites
  serching 4 th lite th blu vase   remembrs all   our lovrs all our
angels n monstrs weev all   bin both n th   danse uv 4givness
is sew enchanting all wayze   th time uv th   unicorn n th strangr
planning langwage is alwayze in desire or   undr langwage un
  spokn hard driving wet n wanting   wettr or th flite from deep
in th kodex kortex template both serabella resound with arousal
n th elixr respons in th brain th endorpheena   relees   th erotik
naytur uv langwage that it is evn partikular at all reminds us uv
th opartikul gendr pronoun wchevr duz it 4 us   alwayze   th fine
possibilitee th potenshul oftn hope is   sew long 2 merg with n
repeet n xakt yuneek each time tho th en   veloping swept up in
th kontinuum uv th tapestreed mirage shimera tho that may cum
latr or during that way uv looking at it trew love th role uv th tem
plates alredee embeddid in our   serabelle front end kortex in
decisyun making wch template mooving in 4   th possessyun
wuns wuns sout caut n wuns walk away aftr red alert with sew
swolln membr fullness inevitablee empties sources lets go n re
gain th potent jestyur eye hed galaxee song ths spirit n th kold
ghost in th barren ivoree room   no wun cud klaim or
cud they tasting th prfekt moment alredee passing thers a word
4 it he she sd mirage its all a dreem isint it evn tho it hurts sure
  duz sumtimez n also makes us sew groovin fine happee get
what u can n lavish upon it b ther with it stand n lay down with
it all thees he sd 2 me squeezin n pinching my nippuls as he did
go on   we dont fit in xsept as we proaktivlee join in embrace th
  frends in2 th kontinuing rhythm not 2 walk on th birth uv love n
being jump in2 it th langwage th wage uv th land th wage uv
being heer on erth whos pulling th strings dew we have outside

our wiring dont we pray 4 wider wiring oh anglikans ar yu all
ths lost like peopul who support war wepons deelrs evreewhr
need 2 get shut down he sd layin down along th rivr uv time
less kissing begin just bcoz we invent gods dusint meen wun
dusint xist is less reel   loves us less konsidr th fine points

agreements imblued with desire points direksyuns also th
trans uv flite in being from temporal th oral temp think abt it
sumtimes estranging endings ar they endings th epik sweep
ther is no onlee ths sew far alwayze mooving evreethings th
line th lettrs want ths want that kontaind they cant get total
ee out th poignansee they spill ovr theyr konfines theyr kon
fitur bold kourage nomenklaytura a nite uv a thousand bleek
nesses alwayze changing yes ths sew far also ring mooving
evreethings th line th lettrs want ths want that our organs th
eye biggr thn our stomach our or gans brains we can nevr
 get it all we ar alredee all enuff   inside yes lost in a debate
detach frends change find yr po sisyun hard2 yu gho on
detaching ar detachd mooving thru   th opickshurs th arbi
traree game killing konstrukts no alleg   ans can i help he
askd is all yu need food medicines thees lettrs dew yu need
 our kulturs texts nest 4 tents r roof 4 try ths A th desire th
desire th desires moaning trimming th glittr inside th walls
w a l l s th glimmring spoon ring dangul dazzul try ths spin
round ring swing out as th canduls get anothr breth evree
 things th line th lettrs animating th sounds words uv layring
sub lingual oftn nevr statid infinitee fitting uv each part s uv
speech sub continent sub konscious sub lingual
as desire is s ar th lettrs animating themselvs th sounds th
words uv layring infinitlee each part p art tarp uv speech can
yu reech that speech 4 me lay mooving as th words n ettrs
ar alive th lettrs words sylabuls each is ar living n ther is
no ending wanting a as being strong is whn we can touch
sum wun elsus mental arousal words   brain bcum alive 4 a
whil yes words lay ring th diskreet diffrens btween rooms
 sum have kold spirits in them othr ghosts thrashing around
looking 4 a key a word names 2 hold on 2 sum rooms ths
warm onlee droping in a soft message 4 sum wun agreed2
leev it ther heer n thn gho on 2 spirit places agen th word

we say 4 things events nuances uv being bcumming chang
ing ar alwayze hanging words both in th spelling n applikay
syuns th pointing n fluiditee turning   in2 konstrukts para
dimes approximaysyuns shellings ar not th reel things ar sym
bols sew changing 4 things also   see shells uv lite roam yu
heet clothes xtrakt sleep covrs th lines heart life hed moistyurs
n th watr gatewayze hed moistyur requitement merit call uv
th provokaysyun cum heer cum in 2 th words its a life sentens
th lantern glows on th porch in ths remark abul kadens a korn
ucopia uv naming storm keep going we   can seel th safetee
words at th top uv th staring tablow who   was th leed trumpet
th 2nd violin n th hiway alwayze turning we ar leeving 4 th leef
just past th landing thats wher th remains uv th heart felt whirl
wind   th suddn rapture uv th familee membr thrusting against
look wher th windows opn keep going pleez yes as yu sd we
can seel th safeteez   theyr ordrings will change our lives build
ings texts message tek nolojee change   whn 2 peopul want 2
merg ther may b no langwages or ther may b dew yu have th
receipe sun burst moon cow thredding   thredding oh its not
redee yet yes sum peopul ar arousd by langwage th love n th
finding th relees uv defining aftr all th hyprbolik ambiguitiez or
what ar yu talking abt th asparagus stalking th klementine wal
rus wardrobe lookd great on him as he walkd   evr neerer th ol
ghostlee tirade n th watr wafer langwage   may cum from th
desire s 2 find hunt wher th bison ar th deer th find hunt th u
angwage whos is whos n whers th work wage   land all th rev
olushyuns agrikultural industrial compewtr cybr nano we go on
changing evolving can we let go uv war wch is   cawsd by th
fighting erupting n go on showing n tell th kostuming   th narra
tivs yet evreething is goldn n th narrativs fall off othrs replay
sing thos kontinuouslee wuns n sew manee th words   th kon
tainrs wuns seeminglee emptee in th shop window all th great
emptee kontainrs standing on top uv each othr each showing
th glistning sew komforting empteeness wher we havint yet put
things that ruin evreething th illusyun uv empteeness th delus
yun uv kleen slate th releef uv it yu know what ium saying she
sighd 2 him siting ther on th sand next 2 his boyfrend yes i get
it he sd i feel if onlee yes she sd its mor wistful thn pragmatik
4 desire th rules uv n parametrs uv desire changing as th allow

ing uv venus multiplisitee broadns bcumming widr th wiring n
yet storeez prsist dew happn tho 2 oftn tragedeez oftn th O n
th store uv piktographik images lettrs thus words dew cum from
multiplsitee can broadn th awareness uv living th detail n th dif
frent views th possibul tendrness words at th top uv th stares
th doorway 2 th muskee murkee attik evreething is goldn up th
steps ovr th kreekee disheveld floor boards wher th gold lettrs
n infinit lettrs ar stord undr th floor bords th yeers feers teers
sayrs storee tellrs whos wher n saying what 2 whom n whos
ths 2 whom cum inside from th klimbing cud i touch yu hold
yu th levls dimensyuns uv konsciousness n preparing   th wo
rds like a well oild n trustid frend yes take us by surprize n we
go furthr inside

       th verbal kostuming as ther is no or universal
desire or langwage as langwage is sew oftn th   langwage uv
wch peopul wch group wch part uv group in self defens or th
rule by role wch kultur wch kontext a coupul kontext a singul
 prson kontext a heterosexist kontext a homo sexual or heter
sexual kontext transgenderd n like that wher   th meening is
 put n put out all groups n kulturs ar sumtimes   inkomprehens
ibul 2 each othr remembring 2 b flexibul 2 hold diffrent uses uv
 langwage s desire eithr stalld deferrd or being aktid upon th
thank th evreethings whn yes all wayze evn all th diffrenses in
finitlee fascinating n uv kours reel non representaysyunal n
representing sumtimes langwage n desire   have no konnex
syun sumtimes is evreething 2 b seen sum times sew thredid
 sew manee dimensyuns uv konsciousness being bcumming
  changing yes yes th th places laces   aces evree singul or
son is diffrent evree gay prson evree   straight prson evree
coupul prson all sew diffrent   n desire lives in evree part s uv
speech inside langwage evreewher inside   we look at each
othr n imagine th taktile preposisyuns uv th courting hunt 4 yu
how our fingrs wud our mouths arms cock wud remembr its
th frendship heer its an amayzing selebate relaysyun ship who
knew it cud happn sew wundrfulee evreewher inside we look
at each othr present n remembring evree word th promise not
 breking them aneething being ther 4 each othr in th present
if thats happning n it is n why not th words that bind in freelee

not wanting 2 b not with th prson or th being prseeving as sew
magikul   all wayze all wayze yes in innosens   peesful mind
sew manee sumtimes sew much processing n   mooving thru
changing all wayze resituating   letting th flow   letting go uv
xpektaysyuns judgments sides what thn mooving thru th pro
cess a apeering in n fading from ther n kommenting meenwhil
mercuree in retrograde   ther is reelee no universal memoree
n th turquois sky n th silvr sky n names n un naming n thrilling
n opn desire in naytur th erotik enerjeez uv th erth treez wind
growing snow blizzard th yu desire wheeling in yr   hed n me
  whn i look at yu 4 hours we hang 2gethr chilling n th nu day
wher dew they get all thees nu dayze from its veree xciting n
full uv sew manee kinds uv magik n desire silentlee as sew
possibul sumtimez watching with watching deer watching th
huge sun set a spirit mooving in th neer red gold crimson dark
ning dusk ovr th spreding lake n koolness redolent uv desire
4 th erth world fulfilling spills ovr us thru th kamoflageing
breething being duende sacrid categoreez dissolv change re
emerg changing kontextul being themselvs as irene karasick sz
a name is a label stiks stones can brek our bones names can
hurt us thees all in langwage blessings n curses fingr pointing
n loving touch words ar erotik as themselvs spilling in n out uv
each othr displaying n oozing thrusting with sultree n needing n
  hot life 2 life th infinit tapestreez uv sound joy greef th words
    hard wet asking akeing grooving lushyus as th lettrs merging
all cumming in2 n out uv each othr n each part uv each yet al
sew evn if its own like ourselvs that poignansee that longing
n resplendent n oftn thrilling touching nd still each uv us n
each lettr itself swelling ther is mor thn wun word 4 th deepr
image translatid thru yu devosyun prayr sub lingual
th blu vase leevs in th wind john keats a thing uv beautee is a
joy 4evr n that is all yu know n all yu need 2 know yes th mes
sage uv th vase 2 b trew in yr line yr vois th choices ar within
th langwage n what yu selekt selekts yu is from   th langwage
th blu vase yr fingr runs ovr its mouth n throat sets itself uprite
u close th window walk tord me th blu vase fuses with yr mouth
on me breething 2gethr in2 th lettr A from whom all lettrs cum

self storage

nowun undrstood

reelee what evreething radiant n breking   down sum uv
thees pomes may show th time he enterd th middul uv th
15th floor he was grateful th pleurtee n ol bleurtee nowun
undrstood reelee th refrain th

th diffrens btween phone sex othrs wer mor sew earleer
or latr n 2 sustain it n mastrbaysyun well   listn i sd phone
sex is sex reel sex th distans is onlee physikal not mental
or spiritual or psychik n th lives ar   announsing gerania
at twelv o klok ohh th blood from th, lilaks er   prfume its
calld heer on erth sankshuaree touch all th fleeting hands
we arous th demons by neglekting 2 plees n love ourselvs
taking care uv ourselvs protekts us its a long   chorus but i
think i can work it in was that sum wanton errant   spell ths
way shake it off i starts with lack uv satisfacksyun in self
dusint it who knows how th insinuation penetrates   he sd
oh well listn i sd n phone sex is konsensual mastrbaysyun
may b all thos if th psychik intrplay is strong enuff n we kno
it can b th emoshyunal angr without angr or   xhaustyun
themselvs in yr hed yr showing up optimism buoyansee
n gud humour nothing sew much   no time 2 write thn n is
it th ideel 2 b afrayd uv waiting 4 th stagnant watr 2 run off
hope it dusint take dayze who has dayze 4 that th sulphur
n wrinkuls thers a lot uv lettrs n charaktrs ar they all beleev
abul nowun undrstood

protein love   goldn

d is 4 darling devotid devastatid sum timez   theyr sew
close pants as ants ar they 2 tite watching realism on tee
vee falling asleep heering icikuls in th beedid walls now
take ths N it seems xcellent like 2 me it   seems sew great
i can slide on it evn thos ths partikular N   nevr tells th ord
inaree trewth oh thers that I sipping in on my N hmmmm
listn its not reelee yres no wun undrstood as th cards kept
raffuling in th raven plenitude   skraptures uv spanish nite
down by th canal ther wer sighs n skreems n low watr moov
ing moans it was th green leef uv time th ripe tomato th

gonads n hot vestibule heels kliking on dice n th changing
shapes faces on th cards nowun reelee undrstood yr wr arint
we xcitid with or dismayd or seriouslee fritend by 4 dayze
2 let go find th name uv th emosyun pin th tail on th is it cum
ming from yu how manee mor neurona can yu blow without
being in th arms uv yr lovr th kompassyunate king   is ther a
        core self or manee aspekting diskreet selvs th needs 4
privasee is evreething anthro po morphik or almost el leon
edgar allan is evreething almost anthro morphik morphitia is la
    A can yu as we surrendr 2 th tunnul yu sd b4 lask word n
        tree love rekalling agen th flin flon arabesk sew gainlee all
wer surprizd n present th taboggan n taybulgram in2 th sandal
wood is evreething almost aNTHROPOMORPHIKAAAAA see
peggys covr nova scotia can gowd get it what its like 2 b us
how oftn konfusing it is squeezd btween lettrs sum uv them
getting returnd all th time nu wuns cumming in oh wow
whos ths xciting yes if we ar god is god also us sure sit
next 2 th atlantik ocean we ar such fish stik toddlrs bside
we ar brout in2 being our minds repelld by n greedee 4
permanens   no wun undrstood tellsum winnows uv a powr
tap that shes ok 2 thers no powr we can sit heer walk heer
    dance heer rage heer lament heer love heer b quiet heer
    n fluidlee th guraffe tango w is 4 wundr

        memoreez cum loading in f letting them go b in th
present its th onlee place espeshulee if wer gud n kind in th
now n havint bin hurt 2 much if neandrthals wer not our
        parents   ar we thn erthlings orphans in space its 2
eezee 2 beleev that th present is th onlee place how thn dew
we effekt change we need 2 moov thru time n space 4 that
    yes ther ar periods uv haunting in our lives sumtimes th
past sumtimes sumthing els remoovs th pillow n th saffron
thees ar almost proscribd by th dna 4 us 2 realize th love
i evn its not cumming 4 us can gowd get in can we allow
gratefulness owww summas wundr evreething that is al
    redee inherent availabul 2 us is gowd pan thru th windo
th lavenning karress whn it cums 2 us th moon swoons thru

tuning in2 th arrogans uv angels   whn we try 2 help
sumwun els whos verbalee abusiv   against us n we
may entr a period uv downfall wrestuling with what 2 let
go uv th prson th program or   th love that isint reelee
love infinit peopuld with wishes n dreems longings being
th lines we remembr thos we   4get or store 2 deeplee
morphika uv th multi fasitid   embar gos barges   th moon
swoons thru th clowds uv angels n dragons   picking sum
peopul up in letting othrs down   i had int writtn 4 sew long
felt great agen 2 b in it th diskreet avoidans uv bad spells
wer they bad or painfulee instruktiv   komplex letting go
beez seez at th dawn th on songing eez   tributareez th
morning serenaid   canoe came rastuls   our strikshurs
n lacks lakes our prepondrances we hem n haw moov thru
th kurtin balkones our egos n mirakuls displays   huge i
desires   in th morning uv th spanish tides all th kondoms
from th nite b4 floating in th rising surf u i love that deva va
va deeev espeshulee from ths window its sew dee n th
brik masonree n th morning gowd gets it how we ar th
troubuld with our design n rippd panteez n undrweer sew
floating 2 shore   we ar nice peopul if we stik 2 getting it
on wer not reelee sew bad whatevr   splashes uv gold
left undr th moon inside th birds uv evreewher
fethrs flashing in th bristuling sand   n th leevings
evn sacrid notes   lavish n lick th watrs wet th
notes writing erasing sumtimes staying
looking   much like aneewher sumwher els n it
life   selvs lites full n th myriad touching
in th face   uv th ghostlee see watrs slapping fettrs
shedding th vineer uv praktikalitees uv wun
uv his shades personae startuld ther drawing on maroon i
wud say th nu kolour uv th walls tuk 7 coats th word 4 ar
eaguls swallows hawks fold in n out uv each othr th moov
mentz uv partikuls breething hunee thru molekular space
strappd in sew off n riding thru th fog n lack uv chattr way
in th beautiful mor north   th hands guide me 2 rest n sleep
thees hands that guide me n care 4 me sew oftn b4

eye   hed   galaxee   song

th face in th heart is th blood
       flowing in th face is th heart mooving
is th blood is th eye opning ar
        th hands 2gethr waking th heart is
    what th spine bcums is th figur
floating
               in th mouth is th heart

speeking in th rivr dansing is th opn
    hand   telling th heart is th love blood
                              mooving
 is th moon singing is th face in th heart is

now is a nowina nowin anowina nowina now
    a nowina bcumming beet ing th heart
                         beeting th figur opn 2
    th sun is th heart beeting opn 2 th sky is
th waves ar singing in th blood is ar th legs ar
  carreeing th heart is th blood mouth sing
  ing is th spine holding   th heart opning

                          2 th fingr tongue
               eeting th heart beeting th
    tongue eeting is th tongue eeting th heart

me n my walking stick

i saw her thru th window i wasint spying eye
just happend 2 b walking by past thees spruce
 she was dansing in her kitchn

                              her arms up n
around her brests hips mooving with th song fire
 rising highr in th stove

                        congo drums singing in th
nite uv ths northern forest cant go out cant go out
 th rainee seesun is down on us gotta stay in kleen
 th walls cook th bred keep th fire going

til its time 2 sleep dont want 2 got sum mor dansing
 2 dew reech thru all ths statik air gonna moov with
it gonna jump with it canduls singing highr klapping
her hands step walking cross th floor

   n th ravens n owls on her cedar roof th thrush
surrendr 2 th mewsik keeping step with her n th
   radio   with ths nite uv th last full

   moon b4 wintr